Gardening in a small space

Cover photograph: contrasting heights, flowers and foliage in a small back garden

Overleaf: A patio garden showing how much colour and interest can be created within a small space
Photographs by Michael Warren

Gardening in a small space

A Wisley Handbook

Robert Pearson

Cassell

The Royal Horticultural Society

Cassell Educational Limited
1 Vincent Square
London, SW1P 2PN
for the Royal Horticultural Society

First published 1980
New edition, fully revised and reset 1986

British Library Cataloguing in Publication Data

Pearson, Robert
 Gardening in a small space. — New ed. —
 (Wisley handbook, v. 38)
 1. Gardening
 I. Title II. Series
 635   SB453

 ISBN 0-304-31131-6

Photographs by Robert Pearson and Michael Warren

Phototypesetting by Franklyn Graphics, Formby
Printed in Hong Kong by Wing King Tong Co. Ltd

Contents

	page
Introduction	6
Putting things in perspective	7
In praise of trees	10
Key conifers	15
Clothing walls and fences	18
Shrubs with a purpose	27
Making the most of roses	35
Perennials for pleasure	38
A selection of bulbous flowers	46
Tubs, pots and window-boxes	50
Raised beds	55
Colour from annuals and biennials	56
Vegetables and fruit	61
A water feature	64

Introduction

Planning and planting a small garden can be an exhilarating experience. But which plants are best suited for the purpose, and what can they be expected to contribute? It is the purpose of this handbook to explore the possibilities. Our views on size are naturally coloured by our own circumstances. To the owner of broad acres a garden of one acre in extent might well be considered a small garden. To the owner of a small courtyard garden almost anything might seem large. The title of this book is intended to cover gardens ranging from patio proportions to something not far short of the size of the typical suburban garden.

Paradoxically, gardens which fall into this category can be more difficult to develop successfully than those of more ample proportions: if you reduce the area involved, plant shapes and sizes, colour blendings and plant associations all take on added significance. More thought needs to be given to the integration of both related and disparate features, with plants being used with more discernment and subtlety. If this sounds a little daunting it is not meant to be. The greatest assets you can have when embarking on this kind of venture are an instinctive feeling for plants and the kind of resourcefulness and imagination which most gardeners can 'pull out of the hat' when the occasion demands.

Pansies such as the Roggli Giant mixture can contribute colour from spring to the end of summer

Putting things in perspective

Like everybody else whose life has revolved around gardening and plants, I have my own ideas on garden design. To some of these I give an airing now, but I am not a garden designer and for a wealth of excellent and succinct advice on this specialised area I would suggest that you consult another handbook in this series, *Plans for Small Gardens*.

My advice to any intending garden maker is to 'hasten slowly'. Rush into things too quickly and it is easy to make bad mistakes, whether you are coping with the development of a new plot or converting an existing garden to meet your interests and tastes. Get the feel of it, soak up the atmosphere and take note of the surroundings immediately beyond your boundary line before even starting to make a plan or buying-in plants to get things moving.

A prime need is to establish at a very early stage the kind of growing medium you have at your disposal. Even in a small garden there can be considerable variations, so find out the pH rating* of the soil over the area generally and, if necessary, improve the physical structure by digging in peat or composted bark fibre.

As to finding the right home for plants in which you are especially interested, if these have clearly defined needs, then it is important to get the measure of your garden's microclimate; that takes a while. Naturally, one can gather quite a lot straight away, but I would want to know more before I settled on a home for, say, a genista or carpeting helianthemums, which need lashings of sunshine, or, in the case of perennials, for hostas, pulmonarias, hellebores or spindly-stemmed, dainty epimediums, all of which prefer a lightly-shaded position.

Never let your heart rule your head by introducing to the garden plants which are plainly unsuited to the conditions which can be offered. It is so easy to do, and quite unnecessary with the vast range of plants available.

One of your priorities should be to evaluate every vertical surface with a plant bed at its base, to assess its possibilities as a growing area, not only for true climbers but for other shrubs which are so well suited for (or need) such positions—the ceanothuses, chaenomeles, *Cotoneaster horizontalis*, Chimonanthus

---

* The symbol pH is used to denote the chemical reaction of the soil. A neutral soil has a pH of 7.0. Below 7.0 is acid, and above alkaline.

praecox, pyracanthas, and the winter-flowering jasmine (*Jasminum nudiflorum*). By gardening upwards in this way you are automatically increasing your growing area and, by varying the levels of interest, adding immeasurably to the attractions of the garden. Sunny, sheltered walls also provide the right conditions for plants of borderline hardiness which one could not contemplate growing elsewhere; for instance, a high proportion of the ceanothuses.

In all but the smallest gardens—which may well be given over to paving interspersed with plant beds and containers—I would always find room for a lawn, however small. Well-tended grass makes a marvellous foil for other features, and even a wide strip (if that is all that can be accommodated) can greatly enhance the appearance of associated features. It soothes the eye in summer and provides colour in winter.

Shrubs are the backbone of the modern garden—easy to look after and an attraction the year round if you plant with a fair degree of skill, taking size into account.

Against this framework of shrubs, trees and taller-growing conifers are the plants which give the garden its distinction and strongest sense of personality. This is true of even quite small trees. By providing focal points of attention and changes in elevation they perform an indispensable service. Only the most minute of gardens should be devoid of them altogether.

For providing a wealth of interest in relatively small areas of ground the bulbous flowers, the herbaceous perennials, the annuals and biennials are invaluable. They can be used to beautify odd corners of the garden and provide a succession of interest around the year.

Vegetables and fruit most certainly come into the reckoning, too; but only in the most space-effective ways. So far as vegetables are concerned, it makes sense to concentrate mostly on salad and reasonably short-term crops of other kinds, and, in fruits, on trained forms of top fruits and, of course, most types of soft fruits; all come in for discussion later. But now back to more general considerations. Earlier, I made the point about using plants with subtlety. Flowers are at the centre of garden enjoyment, but, leaving aside the roses and a handful of other plants, they are in bloom for a relatively short period. That is accepted, but it makes one think more deeply about the advantages which fine-foliaged plants offer the gardener not over-blessed with growing space. They supplement most marvellously the floral displays either for some six months of the growing season or as a permanent feature in the case of the evergreens. Nor is it only a question of colour; shapes and textures can also give a great deal of pleasure. To whet your appetite just think of the contribution which can be made by the evergreen *Elaeagnus pungens* 'Maculata' with its gold-splashed leaves, and *Weigela florida* 'Variegata' with its creamy white leaf variegation and soft pink, foxglove-like flowers in May and June, a delightful assemblage of complementary colours.

Perhaps it is almost inevitable, with space at a premium, that over-planting is something which has taken the edge off the beauty of many a small garden. It should be resisted—most of all because the plants won't like it.

Pyrus salicifolia 'Pendula', a delightful tree for the small garden with its weeping habit and silvery leaves (see p. 10)

In praise of trees

Trees must be accorded an especially honoured place in gardening, just as in the fashioning of the landscape generally. Beautiful, elegant and imposing are some of the adjectives which come immediately to mind when describing their charms. Some, too, like the birches, are even more beautiful in their leafless winter state. However, with these more than with any other group of garden plants, it is necessary for the head to rule the heart. Trees which will ultimately become far too large for the garden should be discounted from the start.

I'm going to start this brief survey with a selection of trees which provide foliage effects. The first of these is the weeping willow-leaved pear, *Pyrus salicifolia* 'Pendula', one of the loveliest small trees I know with its rounded head and canopy of weeping branches clothed with grey, willow-like leaves giving it an almost ethereal appearance in some lights. It is unlikely to exceed 20ft (6m) in height and is usually nearer 15ft (4.5m) tall. White flowers appear in April. It grows well in all soils of reasonable quality, including those which are heavier, wetter and drier than average.

Very easy-going, too, of course, are the birches of which, alas, most grow too large for the size of garden with which we are concerned. Two which can be used are the well-known *Betula pendula* 'Youngii' (Young's weeping birch) and the narrowly upright growing *B. pendula* 'Fastigiata' which is much less often encountered. Like all the birches (greedy feeders by the way), Young's weeping birch has elegance and style, and makes an excellent focal point in a small garden especially when associated with plants like heathers—the winter-flowering *Erica herbacea* (*E. carnea*) varieties only, if you have a limy soil—which have a natural affinity with it. *Betula pendula* 'Fastigiata', which makes a narrow column 25ft (7.5m) or a little more tall, I've seen used most effectively in a small front garden given over mostly otherwise to lawn.

If you have a garden at the upper end of the size range, the Swedish birch, *B. pendula* 'Dalecarlica', with its pendulous branches bearing light green, deeply cut leaves, could be considered. It is almost certain in time to reach a height of 40ft (12m), but a mitigating factor is that birches, with their airy framework of branches, are not trees which greatly inhibit light.

Not many gardeners, in my experience, seem to be aware of the existence of that charming little weeping willow, *Salix purpurea* 'Pendula', even though it is the one by far the best suited to small gardens. This standard form of the purple osier reaches a height of little more than 9 to 10ft (2.7–3m) and a spread of a few feet less.

It is only since the early 1970s that *Robinia pseudacacia* 'Frisia' has become well known. This golden-yellow-foliaged false acacia creates a glorious splash of colour to a height of some 30ft (9m) right through from spring to autumn, when the colouring changes before leaf fall to a pleasing amber shade. With a width of about 15ft (4.5m) it can, moreover, be incorporated into many a planting scheme. Culturally, it will do well in a wide range of soils, although it must be exposed to plenty of sunshine to bring out the colour at its best. 'Frisia' has, however, a skeleton in its cupboard: its wood is brittle and branch snapping is a common occurrence if one is imprudent enough to plant it in a position where wind can set it creaking and straining. A sheltered position is a necessity.

A tree one links naturally in one's thoughts with the robinia is the thornless *Gleditsia triacanthos* 'Sunburst'. Its size is roughly similar to that of the last mentioned and it is also accommodating culturally. However, it doesn't hold its leaf colour like 'Frisia' and, while the fern-like leaves begin a glorious golden yellow, this gradually changes to pure green as the season advances. On the other hand, it has a rather better shape than the robinia (whose branches can look a little ragged) and it does not suffer from brittle wood. Both trees are tolerant of air pollution.

Only about half the height of the last two—and slow to put on growth— is a very striking sycamore named *Acer pseudoplatanus* 'Brilliantissimum', a gorgeous sight in spring when the leaves open a beautiful shrimp pink, which gradually gives way to greenish-yellow and, finally, to pure green. This needs to be grown in a position where the light will strike it at the right angle. So, too, does the lovely snake-bark maple *A. pensylvanicum*, but only if you can provide it with a lime-free soil. It has beautiful white- and green-striped bark and, for a brief spell in autumn, butter-yellow leaf colouring. Perhaps the best of all the maples for autumn colour, though, is the Japanese maple, *A. palmatum* 'Osakazuki' which assumes at that time brilliant red hues. Like all the *palmatum* varieties, however, it needs a position out of cold winds. Neither of this pair will usually exceed 15ft (4.5m) in height and, like all the maples, they appreciate a rather good, nicely moist but well-drained soil in which to grow.

Most hollies rank as trees rather than shrubs and for year-round display these reliable but rather slow-growers are unsurpassed. My favourite is the male (and therefore non-berrying) *Ilex aquifolium* 'Golden Queen', some 15ft (4.5m) tall and 8 to 10ft (2.4–3m) in width. It shouts out a message of good cheer, especially in winter, with its mass of prickly leaves an amalgam of green and rich golden-yellow (on the margins), with some grey suffusions with the green. Another holly, somewhat smaller growing, is 'Handsworth New Silver', with leaves of green and grey margined with creamy white. When carrying its bright red berries it is very eye-catching indeed. Remember that with female hollies there needs to be a male form growing reasonably close to get a good set of berries.

Turning to flowering trees, it is the ornamental cherries (*Prunus*) which generally excite the most interest. A whole host of them are suitable for most small gardens, but I must restrict my choice to just a handful. One of the loveliest in my opinion is *P.* 'Shimidsu Sakura' which, for several weeks in late spring, captivates with its pure white, double flowers (these open from pink-tinged buds). It grows some 12 to 15ft (3.6–4.5m) tall and so can be found a home in many a small space open to plenty of sunshine, which is something that all flowering cherries need. Its shape, too, is beguiling, for it makes a well-rounded head with the lowermost branches sweeping down almost to ground level. A cherry of fully weeping habit is 'Kiku Shidare Sakura', similar in height to the last and with deep pink, double blooms in April.

Where lateral space is not available but height is, a tree is advantageous to the overall design. The natural choice of cherry would be 'Amanogawa' which grows up to 20ft (6m) tall but not more than 8 ft (2.5m) wide and often quite a lot less. This becomes a pillar of shell pink in late April and May. With rather more lateral room, *Prunus × hillieri* 'Spire' might appeal even more, for this grows up to 25ft (7.5m) tall and up to 10ft (3m) wide bearing soft pink blooms in April and providing really good, rich red leaf colour in autumn.

In the context of this book I would consider the autumn cherry, *P. subhirtella* 'Autumnalis' well worth your attention, too, for, despite its name, it does bear its small, semi-double white flowers right through from November to March, except when hard weather intervenes. These are very pretty seen as a network of white against the bare branches. It will make a tree of rather spreading habit to 20ft (6m) or so and much the same in height.

The ornamental crabs appeal to me, especially shapely little *Malus × robusta* in its form known as the Yellow Siberian. This is a profusion of white blossom for a time in spring, and then from early autumn is highly decorative with its long-persisting yellow fruits. Its height and spread is usually well under 20ft (6m). Again, there is a good columnar variety in 'Van Eseltine', which makes a tree some 20ft (6m) tall on which semi-double, shell-pink flowers

Acer palmatum 'Osakazuki', a large bush or rounded small tree, provides a striking splash of colour in autumn (see p. 11)

open from red buds in May and yellow fruits follow in early autumn. Especially beautiful in May, for its pale pink to white flowers opening from rosy red buds, is the Japanese crab *Malus floribunda*, which makes a round-headed tree from 15ft (4.5m) tall and wide.

Likewise, there are numerous excellent mountain ashes (*Sorbus*), which belong to the Aucuparia section of the genus. Quite delightful is *Sorbus vilmorinii*, only 15ft (4.5m) or so tall and less wide, with a neat habit, pretty fern-like foliage and, in autumn, pendent clusters of fruits, which start off red and gradually change to pink and finally white with pink suffusions. Very highly regarded also is the larger 'Joseph Rock' (up to 25ft

13

[7.5m] tall but considerably less in width) which has fine autumn leaf colour and fruits starting off a rather pale yellow but deepening in colour as they mature.

The flowering cherries, ornamental crabs and mountain ashes all grow well in any average soil (including those of an alkaline nature), given good drainage. The first two need sunny positions, but the last are satisfactorily grown in either sunshine or light shade.

Unquestionably the best magnolia for small gardens is *Magnolia stellata*, to which you will find reference in the chapter on shrubs (see p. 27), but it is impossible to ignore the delightful *M. × soulangiana* which is such a wonderful sight in April when the goblet-shaped blooms, suffused with purple on the outside of the petals and white within, open on the bare branches. And, of course, flowering continues well into May, when the leaves are unfolding. The reservation about it in the practical context is its spread, for it makes a low-branched tree of, perhaps, eventually 25 to 30ft (7.5–10m) tall and as much in width, with the growths coming almost to the ground.

Magnolia × soulangiana and its varieties are, alas, not suitable for limy soils. What suits them best is a good well-drained loamy soil which is retentive of moisture. Don't plant in a frost pocket either or the blooms will suffer. Despite what I have said about their size, *M. × soulangiana* and its forms are often seen as main features in town and city gardens and, as is well known, they have a high resistance to atmospheric pollution.

Let's finish with a broom and a laburnum, namely *Genista aetnensis*, the Mount Etna broom, which is more often grown as a large shrub than a single-stemmed tree, and *Laburnum × watereri* 'Vossii'. Both are much to be valued for bringing strong yellows—the most cheerful of all colours—into the garden at different parts of the summer.

In fact, the Mount Etna broom can be extraordinarily useful if you want to give a planting scheme height without casting much shade. Grown on a clear stem, it will carry its elegant top-hamper of whippy growths to a height of up to 20ft (6m) and be really spectacular when the racemes of golden-yellow pea flowers are borne in July and August. If medium-sized shrubs are grown around its base the rather gaunt appearance of the tree will be entirely masked. Late May and early June is the time when *Laburnum × watereri* 'Vossii' produces its profusion of long, rich yellow racemes of flowers. Expect it to have a height eventually of 30ft (9m) and a width of 20ft (6m). The genista likes full exposure to sunshine and, for preference, a lightish soil. The laburnum will be happy in any average soil in sunshine or light shade.

Key conifers

Conifers fascinate me. These are plants where shapes, colours and textures so often combine in a specific species or variety to provide us with something having dramatic impact. Keeping within the size limitations imposed by the theme of this book, one need look no further for an example of this than the conical-shaped blue spruce, *Picea pungens* 'Koster', with its tier on tier of branches densely packed with silvery-blue leaves. Eventually, this will reach 30ft (9m) or so in height and perhaps 15ft (4.5m) wide. It's a marvellous associate for heathers and, of course, for growing with others of its kind—conifers which will provide sharp contrasts in form like the prostrate, grey-green *Juniperus horizontalis* 'Bar Harbor', which makes a mass of whippy stems and provides an attractive ground-covering carpet, or maybe a small and slow-growing yew like *Taxus baccata* 'Semperaurea', the yellow of whose foliage varies in intensity from summer to winter and which will not reach its full height of about 6ft (1.8m) for many years.

You will have to decide whether you want to have a conifer which, although not growing very wide (perhaps about 12ft [3.6m]) will in time be nearer 40ft (12m) than 30ft (9m) in height. In certain circumstances it could still have a place in quite a small garden. If that is so, then a golden conifer to consider—for a sunny position, which all yellow-foliaged conifers need to bring out their colour—could be *Chamaecyparis lawsoniana* 'Lanei', which carries its growths in dense sprays and which, while presenting a golden-yellow face to the world, is a greeny yellow underneath. It is especially effective in winter when such warm colours are a real need. Other golden conifers are *Cupressus macrocarpa* 'Goldcrest' (but only for a sheltered position) and *Taxus baccata* 'Fastigiata Aurea', the form of the Irish yew which has green leaves with yellow margins. The first grows eventually to about 30ft (9m), the second to 15ft (4.5m).

You could also be interested in two other Lawson cypresses—*Chamaecyparis lawsoniana* 'Columnaris', which makes a narrow column of glaucous blue, tight-packed, vertical sprays and, after ten years, is unlikely to be more than 8ft (2.5m) tall (and twice that in 20 years), and 'Pembury Blue', raised in a Kent nursery some 40 years ago and popular on the Continent but only now getting into its stride here. 'Pembury Blue' has an attractive conical habit and will probably be about 12ft (3.6m) tall some ten years from planting, although eventually reaching some 30ft (9m) in height. In a small garden, however, such slowness of growth can, quite often, be a decided advantage.

An interesting introduction from the United States which also brings blue into the garden is *Juniperus scopulorum* 'Blue Heaven', pyramidal in habit and eventually around 20ft (6m) tall but only half that height after ten years. If you want the equivalent of an exclamation mark, however, to set off a low planting, then the pencil-slim *Juniperus virginiana* 'Skyrocket' could well be the answer, faster growing than the last and never becoming much over 1 to 2ft (30–60cm) in width, even though its full height can be as much as 20ft (6m). It has greyish blue colouring.

An old friend to many gardeners is *Thuja occidentalis* 'Rheingold', a conifer of conical habit with yellow foliage of a very sympathetic shade (often described by nurserymen as old gold). This turns to a pleasing shade of bronzy gold after the arrival of winter. Much the same old-gold colouring is a winter feature, too, of a beautiful small thuja of Dutch raising—*T. occidentalis* 'Sunkist', which is rich yellow during the summer months. It should prove a popular choice for a sunny position, only a few feet tall after a considerable number of years. 'Rheingold' may eventually reach a height of as much as 10ft (3m), but it is more likely to be 5 or 6ft (1.5–1.8m), and 'Sunkist' perhaps 3½ to 4ft (1–1.2m). For more about some of the best small conifers see the chapter on plants for containers (p. 50).

Pinus mugo, the dwarf mountain pine, is much used in gardens in Switzerland—not unnaturally as it is a native of the mountains of central Europe. A good dwarf form like 'Gnom' is a handsome sight with its characteristic bristly growths of dark green; globe shaped, and taking many years to reach a maximum height and width of 5 to 6ft (1.5–1.8m), it is notably good at coping with limy soils. Another extremely attractive form of the dwarf mountain pine is 'Mops', with a dense, bun-like habit and slow growth. It is usually only about 1½ft (45cm) tall by 2ft (60cm) wide after ten years. Another of small size which could be of interest is a form of the native Scots pine, *Pinus sylvestris* 'Beuvronensis', dome shaped and handsome and with lighter coloured foliage than the last. It will reach much the same size as 'Gnom' (or a little more), again after many years.

As to the growing conditions suitable for the different genera, junipers will grow well in any soil of reasonable quality, including soils of a chalky nature (indeed they are the best conifers for such conditions, followed, perhaps, by the yews, varieties of *Chamae-cyparis lawsoniana* and the thujas, although none except the yews are going to take too kindly to really thin soils of this kind). They

Chamaecyparis lawsoniana 'Columnaris' can make a fine feature in a small space

need plenty of exposure to sunshine. The chamaecyparis and cupressus varieties do well in most well-drained soils of average quality, given shelter from cold winds and good light conditions. The cypresses are of variable degrees of hardiness, and *macrocarpa* varieties like the one mentioned can certainly be damaged if exposed to cold, drying winds. They are excellent for growing in seaside districts in more favoured parts of the country. The cypresses also need to be planted young to get them off to a good start.

The yews are very accommodating, both with regard to soils and available light, doing well in sunshine or shade. Chalk soils are taken in their stride by yews, as I've already remarked, and *Taxus baccata* is endemic to such conditions as a British native. Piceas, however, like good, moisture-retentive but well-drained soils and are best kept off very thin, chalky soils. The pines need good light and clean air but will do well on poorish soils and some, like *Pinus mugo*, are very good on limy soils.

Clothing walls and fences

There are many fine plants to be grown either against house walls or the surfaces of outbuildings or fences; so many, in fact, that I can only cover those which, in my view, have some special significance. Some are real aristocrats, others good, solid workaday plants which are worth every inch of space given over to them. Climbing and wall plants (note the distinction, for most of the plants discussed here are not climbers but shrubs which happen to be ideal for—or need, if they are a bit tender—this kind of treatment) add much to the attractions of the garden.

Let's start with *Fremontodendron* 'California Glory', for this is a splendid shrub which is becoming more and more popular. It is semi-evergreen and bears lobed leaves of a dull green colour which make a marvellous foil for the waxy-looking, bright yellow flowers, borne from late May to July. These are single and cup-shaped at first, gradually flattening as they age. You can expect it to reach a height of 12ft (3.6m) or so, and it must be given a home on a warm, sunny wall.

I don't know who first thought of giving fremontodendron that beautiful mallow *Abutilon vitifolium* as a companion, but it was an inspired move and one taken up, I'm glad to say, by quite a lot of other garden owners. This mallow likes exactly the same conditions as the fremontodendron, including the provision of a preferably light, well-drained soil, which can, if necessary, be of a chalky nature. It is soft-wooded, has extremely attractive vine-like, grey-green leaves, and needs every bit of cossetting it can be given. Soft mauve, funnel-shaped flowers are borne in the period May to July, and there is also a superior form, named 'Veronica Tennant', with blooms of even better quality. It may grow a few feet taller than the fremontodendron. It is not a long-lived plant—nor is fremontodendron for that matter—and it is necessary to say that a vicious winter is likely to sound its death knell.

The above-mentioned abutilon is deciduous; *Abutilon megapotamicum*, also extremely beautiful, is semi-evergreen and quite different. Again, however, it is a plant for a warm, sheltered wall facing south or west, when it can be expected to cover an area of about 6ft by 6ft (1.8 × 1.8m) with its whippy, thin growths. It has very elegant leaves, ovate and sharp pointed and of a fresh green colour, which seem exactly right for the dainty flowers borne from April to autumn. The flower consists of a red calyx, yellow petals and purple stamens, and has an air of great delicacy.

To see the flowers hanging in quantity on a well-grown specimen is the most lovely of sights.

Let's remain on the warm, sheltered side of the house and see what else we might grow there. Staying among the 'big boys', perhaps it would be that lovely broom from Morocco with the pineapple-scented flowers, *Cytisus battandieri*, or, a great favourite of mine, the Californian *Garrya elliptica*. This last one can be grown on a wall of any aspect if you are prepared to risk the leaf damage which can result from exposure to extremely cold, searing winds in the worst of winter weather.

Cytisus battandieri will easily attain a height and spread of 15ft (4.5m) in warm conditions, and it will delight with its handsome, silvery grey, trifoliate leaves with a silky veneer, especially when in July the plump, upstanding racemes of golden yellow flowers put in an appearance. Like all the brooms it is happiest on lightish, very well-drained soils, and is perfectly at home, too, on alkaline soils.

Garrya elliptica is evergreen and will reach in time a height of 20ft (6m) or so, with a similar width. The dark green, shiny leaves, oval to roundish in shape, greyish on their undersides, are in this case also a splendid foil for the showy catkins, which are borne in January and February. These are greyish green in colour and it is important to make sure that you obtain the male form, for this has longer and altogether more impressive catkins than the female, at least 6 inches (15cm) long. As they are carried in great quantity on a good specimen, this shrub can be a wonderful sight in mid-winter—a veritable static waterfall of soft colouring.

The lovely, evergreen *Clematis armandii* most certainly needs the protection of a warm, sunny wall to succeed for, although it is vigorous, it is susceptible to weather damage. Don't be put off, however, for *C. armandii* is a beautiful species, climbing to a height of 20 to 30ft (6–9m) and furnishing itself with a wealth of dark green, very handsome trifoliate leaves with sharp-pointed ends. Then, in April (late March sometimes) arrive the clusters of highly attractive creamy white flowers. 'Apple Blossom' is a fine form, with white, pink-suffused flowers. 'Snowdrift' is a pure white variety, also much to be desired.

Clematis of all kinds love alkaline soils and, as every gardener knows, they like to have their roots kept cool while their top growth is in sunshine. Shade for the roots is easily arranged, of course, by growing leafy, low plants around their base—or by placing flat stones over the root area. On the whole, they are easy-going about aspect, the majority of the large-flowered varieties being very versatile and growing well in a northerly-facing position, provided it is not overshadowed by trees or buildings which would cut down the light value to unacceptable proportions. Indeed, less direct sunshine can be an asset in the case of those varieties whose blooms deteriorate quickly if over-exposed in this way. I shall return to the clematis later in the chapter. Now more suggestions for sunny, sheltered walls and other surfaces.

Blue is a colour less well represented than reds and yellows in the garden. It suggests coolness and elegance and, combined with soft colours like pinks and greys, can have enormous charm. Clematis produce lovely offerings of this kind and one thinks also of the wisterias, most desirable of climbers; but for the moment let us concentrate on the genus *Ceanothus*. Ceanothuses generally are beautiful plants, and I have an especially soft spot for the low-growing, evergreen *C. thyrsiflorus repens*, which grows no more than 3 to 4ft (0.9–1.2m) tall but has a spread of 6 to 9ft (1.8–2.7m). It smothers itself with pale blue flowers in May, has attractive, small, glossy green leaves and is ideal for planting under a ground-floor window in the kind of position which provides sunshine and warmth. A useful plant for many gardens.

Ceanothus thyrsiflorus itself is one of the hardiest of the evergreen ceanothuses (all of which are less hardy than the deciduous kinds, of which 'Gloire de Versailles' is by far the best known) and is likely to be encountered often on warm walls, making a marvellous show in May and June with its quantities of pale blue flowers contrasting with the dark green, shiny foliage. It can be anything from 10 to 20ft (3–6m) in height, depending on the circumstances.

Many *Ceanothus* varieties are worth investigating. 'Delight', for instance, is a fine hybrid for May flowering, covering a space of up to 20ft by 20ft (6 × 6m) with a haze of rich blue. Again, there could be a place in your garden for the rather smaller growing 'Autumnal Blue', for this carries its soft blue flowers from July to October.

The hardier deciduous kinds can often be given a free-standing position, provided that this is well-sheltered from cold winds and is open to sunshine, and so leave wall space for other plants more in need of protection. Ceanothuses prefer lighter soils of good quality and really good drainage. They will tolerate alkaline soils but most draw the line at being asked to make do with thin, chalky soils.

Soils of this last type are not suitable either for perhaps the loveliest climber of all—the wisteria, in all other ways so accommodating if given warmth, sunshine and shelter from cold winds. Wisterias really appreciate a rich loam in which to spread their roots. Both the violet-blue Japanese wisteria, *W. floribunda*, and its Chinese counterpart, *W. sinensis*, have white forms (named

Viburnum × juddii, a bushy deciduous shrub which is free-flowering and easily cultivated (see p. 23)

'Alba') which can look beautiful in the right setting, but blue, or some shade from mauve to lilac, somehow seems more right for this flower. The most spectacular wisteria is undoubtedly *W. floribunda* 'Macrobotrys', which bears racemes of bluish lilac blooms measuring up to 3ft (90cm) long. On house walls, climbing into trees, on pergolas, even as free-standing specimens, they are a dream in May and June when in full flower—and the fragrance is delicious in the right weather conditions. On walls, these climbers can have huge spreads, of course (*W. sinensis* in particular), but as they have such handsome foliage, quite apart from their flowers, that need not be a disincentive.

Some of the most spectacular vines are also greedy in their territorial demands. If you have the space, then *Vitis coignetiae* is a very handsome vine to grow and a glorious sight in autumn when the leaves turn to fiery shades of red. Likewise, that other superb autumn-colourer, the true Virginia creeper, *Parthenocissus quin-*

21

quefolia. Otherwise, plump for the more restrained but still strong-growing *Parthenocissus henryana*, a most beautiful vine with leaves made up of three to five leaflets, dark green in colour and with silvery white and pink veining—colouring brought out most strongly when the plant is given light shade. This, too, has good autumn colouring, the leaves turning then to bright red shades.

I would suggest that you find space for the winter sweet, *Chimonanthus praecox*, if you can provide it with a snug home. This produces its waxy-looking flowers on the bare wood for several weeks at the turn of the year—but only after the plant has reached some degree of maturity. The wait is worthwhile, for the flowers of pale yellow, suffused with purple at the base of the petals, have exquisite scent. A sprig cut and placed in a warm room overnight will fill it with fragrance. Again, it is a plant for a warm, sheltered south- or west-facing wall where it can be expected to cover an area of something like 6ft by 6ft (1.8 × 1.8m). Any good, well-drained soil is suitable for it, and it does especially well on chalky soils. There is a variety named 'Luteus' with larger flowers without the purple marking.

For growing in a bed against a south- or west-facing wall there is also the Mexican orange blossom, *Choisya ternata*, which makes a bush some 6 to 8ft (1.8–2.4m) tall and bears exquisitely fragrant white flowers in terminal clusters in late spring. These are borne against a background of glossy-textured, trifoliate leaves.

If you have lime-free soil, then room should be found for at least one camellia, ideal candidates for west- and north-facing wall beds provided these are not of the kind which dry out excessively. (See also the Wisley handbook on camellias.) I'm thinking in terms of the varieties of *Camellia japonica* and *C. × williamsii* hybrids, particularly the latter, for not only are the varieties superb flowerers, but in addition they have the very good habit of dropping their spent blooms; the *japonica* hold on to their flowers in a rather untidy way, necessitating quite frequent picking over. On this question of aspect, south is not suitable because that provides conditions that are too 'hot', while an eastern aspect allows the early-morning sun to strike frost-rimmed blooms and so damage the petals. North aspects, as I've remarked, are suitable, but not if the plant (or plants) is going to be subjected to cold, drying winds. West is best of all for by the time the sun gets round to that side of the house or garden wall, even in high summer, it will have lost a good deal of its strength.

In the *japonica* varieties, all of which have good foliage of rich, glossy green, there are those with single and others with semi-double, anemone-form and fully double flowers. The choice is very wide. A particular favourite of mine is 'Lady Clare', which bears semi-double blooms of a very appealing soft pink on a bush with rather pendulous, spreading branches. Others are 'Elegans' with rose-pink flowers of anemone-form shape, 'Adolphe Audusson' which bears scarlet, semi-double blooms and 'Donckelarii' with its red blooms often flecked with white.

The *williamsii* hybrids derive on one side from *C. japonica* (the other parent is *C. saluenensis*) and this shows through in the excellence of their foliage. The most famous of these is undoubtedly 'Donation', and very beautiful it is with its rose-pink, semi-double flowers so freely borne. Another with an upright habit like 'Donation' is the variety 'J. C. Williams' which has single blooms of blush pink, again borne with great freedom. It can, moreover, often flower early in the new year, given the right conditions. 'November Pink' will also live up to its name with that same proviso. However, later winter and early spring must be considered 'camellia time', generally speaking. I don't think we value enough the decorative qualities of the foliage at other times of the year; it can make a telling foil for other plants. As to size, you must expect all of them to attain a height of at least 6ft (1.8m) or more.

Viburnum × juddii is a marvellous medium-sized shrub for April–May flowering. The flowers are white with a pink tinge and very highly fragrant. Making a shapely bush some 5ft (1.5m) tall and rather more wide, it benefits from the protection of a wall, aspect not being very important. Like all viburnums it needs plenty of moisture in the soil.

For clothing a north or west wall give a thought to that distinctive forsythia, *F. suspensa* (or its variety *sieboldii*). The very flexible growths do need to be trained, but with this attention it will cover a space 12ft (3.6m) tall and wide and be a source of much pleasure when bearing its pale yellow flowers in March and early April. It has no special soil needs.

Equally accommodating are chaenomeles (japonicas or Japanese quinces as they are popularly called) and pyracantha. Of the chaenomeles one of my favourites is 'Moerloosii', which bears either single or semi-double white blooms, suffused with pink; another is the well-known 'Knap Hill Scarlet', with single, orange-red flowers. Both are March–April flowering. These will make trained specimens some 8ft (2.4m) tall and considerably more across. If something rather shorter is needed, then the choice should be 'Simonii', which bears deep red flowers and has a height of less than 3ft (90cm).

The pyracanthas, on the other hand, will, in many cases, as with the well-known *Pyracantha coccinea* 'Lalandei', reach almost up to the eaves of the house. With its orange-red berries borne in prodigious quantities, it is certainly a variety which gives good value. 'Orange Glow', with orange berries, is perhaps even better. The American-raised 'Mohave' has orange-red berries and especially fine foliage and is also resistant to both scab and fire blight, which can afflict this genus of evergreens. The yellowish orange-berried 'Teton', with a notably upright habit of growth and good glossy-foliage densely borne, is also much to the fore these days.

It would be unthinkable not to mention also that most useful and popular of wall shrubs, *Cotoneaster horizontalis*, the herring-bone cotoneaster. It is best in a sunny place but will do well in any position, producing masses of long-lasting berries in autumn and putting on a fine foliage display when the leaves turn to fiery red before falling. Growing to 3ft (90cm) tall at most, it has a spread of more than 6ft (1.8m). It has no special soil needs.

Nothing is better for covering a fence than the honeysuckles, and the best-known of these are the early Dutch and late Dutch varieties, respectively *Lonicera periclymenum* 'Belgica' and *L. periclymenum* 'Serotina', for flowering in the first and second halves of summer. Both are extremely free-flowering and their purplish-red and yellow blooms are very fragrant. Like clematis, they need a cool root run and prefer plenty of sunshine on their top growth. However, they will also do well in light shade.

A very choice but scentless honeysuckle, which needs to be given a home where it will not be exposed to the full force of summer sunshine, is *L. tragophylla*, from western China. The lack of scent is more than made up for by the beauty of the blooms, for they are golden yellow, narrow cylindral in shape and borne in clusters of between 10 and 20 in June and July on a plant which can climb to a height of 15ft (4.5m). A loamy soil of really good quality is needed to get this plant to do well.

Then there is that splendid foliage honeysuckle, *L. japonica* 'Aureo-reticulata' (the small flowers are of little decorative value), which produces a mass of semi-evergreen small leaves, oval in shape, which are coloured bright green with an intricate network of yellow veining.

Another splendid group of plants are the ivies, and particularly the variegated form of the Persian ivy, *Hedera colchica* 'Dentata Variegata', which bears a mass of large heart-shaped leaves in a mixture of green and grey with a broad irregular margin of creamy white. Also very attractive and popular is *H. colchica* 'Sulphur Heart' (also known incorrectly as 'Paddy's Pride'), in which the leaves are heavily marked from the centre with yellow and paler green than the rest of the leaf. Of the numerous *H. helix* varieties (*helix* being, of course, the common ivy) the best in my

Camellia japonica 'Lady Clare' (left) and *C.* × *williamsii* 'J. C. Williams' (right), two old favourites with attractive glossy green foliage to set off their lovely blooms (see p. 23)

opinion is 'Buttercup', which has golden foliage—the leaves do, however, gradually turn green with age. 'Silver Queen' is another variety of excellence, this having leaves margined with white. These ivies are extremely easy to grow. (See also the Wisley handbook on ivies.)

So, too, is the lovely winter-flowering jasmine, *Jasminum nudiflorum*. It can be grown on walls of any aspect, and only the most severe weather will cause it to falter in its task of bringing cheer between November and February with its bright yellow flowers. Too often, however, it is left to make a veritable tangle of growth with its whippy stems. It needs proper training right from the start, and annual pruning thereafter, in March. This is straightforward enough: just remove any dead or weak wood and cut out the laterals which have flowered so that new shoots (which form readily along the main growths) can take over to provide the flower in the following winter. It will reach a height of 8 to 20ft (2.4–3m).

I said earlier that I would return to the clematis family. Few climbers could possibly be more rewarding than the lovely *Clematis montana*, whether in its variety 'Rubens', rosy-pink; 'Elizabeth', pale pink; 'Tetrarose', lilac-pink; or, my favourite, 'Grandiflora', pure white. May is the month of glory for *montana*, with 'Grandiflora' coming into flower in the latter part of May and 'Rubens' carrying on into June. It is not uncommon for these clematis to climb to a height of 30ft (9m) on a wall. They are easy to grow and will do well on a north wall open to plenty of light.

For late summer and early autumn flowering a delightful species is available in *C. orientalis*, this bearing yellow bell-shaped flowers with sepals so thick it has been dubbed the 'orange-peel' clematis, and silky seed heads of a silvery colour which appear in early autumn with the last of the flowers. 'Bill Mackenzie' is a splendid form of the species. Both have attractive, pale green, fern-like foliage. Much more widely grown for late summer and early autumn flowering is *C. tangutica* from central Asia, a close relative of *C. orientalis* with yellow, lantern-shaped flowers and silky, silvery seed heads.

The large-flowered varieties are many and varied—from such superb early-season flowerers as the mauvish pink 'Nelly Moser', which has a carmine bar on its petals, purple-blue 'The President' and lilac-blue 'W. E. Gladstone', to later-flowering varieties such as purple 'Jackmanii Superba' and pink 'Hagley Hybrid'. (See also the Wisley handbook on clematis.)

Reluctantly, for so many good plants have remained outside this all-too-brief survey, I must conclude with two doughty self-clinging climbers of great size and much vigour. These are *Hydrangea petiolaris* and *Polygonum baldschuanicum*, the Russian vine (it comes from southern Tadzhikstan) or the mile-a-minute plant. Both are ideal for scrambling up into tall trees, often to dizzy heights, but I am thinking of them as coverers of bare walls, especially those difficult to fill well with many other plants.

Hydrangea petiolaris, which comes from Japan, is a very handsome plant indeed when it is bearing its huge panicles of dull white flowers in early summer. Each of these consists of a flat corymb of tiny dullish white flowers surrounded by quite a small number of much larger, pure white, sterile, flowers; these can be 10 inches (25cm) across. The leaves are large and round to ovate with pointed ends and dark green colouring. The best home for it is a lightly shaded wall. North walls are perfectly suitable; south facing walls not at all.

Polygonum baldschuanicum is a plant which is happy to grow in a position with any aspect, in any ordinary soil, and it is really extraordinarily attractive when viewed, close to, in flower. It blooms from July until the frosts arrive. The white, pink-flushed flowers are borne in huge panicles which, collectively, have a billowing lightness and grace. The leaves are attractive, too, ovate to heart-shaped and of a fresh green colour. Don't underrate it just because it is so easy and accommodating.

Shrubs with a purpose

Sometimes there can be an embarrassment of riches; I am sure that many a garden maker has so thought when confronted with the wealth of shrubs in a garden centre or in a nursery. Of course, there can never be too many, and the fear until quite recently was that there would be too few, with many fine plants for which there is a limited demand gradually disappearing from nurserymen's lists. But now we seem to be seeing far more choice plants being offered. Major private gardens open to the public also often have plant stalls at which less commonly seen plants can be obtained. My task now is to remind you of (or introduce you to) some of the shrubs which, collectively, will provide you with pleasure and interest around the year.

So let's start at the dawn of the new year and carry through to the following Christmas. I believe that many of us get enormous pleasure from our gardens in winter. What fun it is to potter around in the garden on a January morning, when the sun is shining and conifer colours sparkle and contrast with the filigree of branches provided by leafless trees, and to stop and marvel at the curiously contorted petals of the Chinese witch hazel, *Hamamelis mollis*, or the spread of colour from winter-flowering heaths, varieties of *Erica herbacea (carnea)*.

Indeed, the *herbacea* varieties make an admirable starting point, for the earliest of these to come into bloom, like the dwarf 'King George' with rosy-pink, brown-tipped blooms, are well into their flowering period by the time the new year comes. And January sees the flowering of that marvellous pair, 'Springwood White' and 'Springwood Pink', both of trailing habit and splendid ground coverers. Both have prominent brown anthers and, in the pure white 'Springwood White' in particular, this adds much to the attractions of the blooms. 'Springwood Pink' is a rose-pink colour. I'm particularly fond, too, of the low-growing 'Vivellii', which has carmine-red blooms (borne in February and March) with dark green foliage which turns to bronze in winter. A more recently introduced variety is 'Myretoun Ruby', which bears ruby-red flowers from February to April and has dark green foliage to provide a strong contrast. Another variety with much to contribute is 'Ann Sparkes', which has deep yellow foliage (tipped with dull red in winter) and purplish-red flowers from February to April. Taller than most at 12 inches (30cm) (most fall within the 6 to 10 inches [15–26cm] range) is 'Pink Spangles'. This has fine deep pink flowers from January to March and covers the ground especially well.

The *Erica herbacea* varieties flower at a time of year when colour is especially welcome and are among the few heaths and heathers which will tolerate limy soils. If you have a neutral or acid soil, then you can take your pick from the enormous range of varieties of *Erica, Calluna* and *Daboecia* which will give colour throughout the year, with careful planning. These, mixed with a few choice conifers to provide contrast and height variations, can be an enormous pleasure. (See also the Wisley handbook on heaths and heathers.)

The winter-flowering heaths integrate splendidly with the Chinese witch hazel mentioned earlier, and the variety which I would suggest growing is *Hamamelis mollis* 'Pallida', a sulphur-yellow form which flowers especially freely, bearing its curious flowers with strap-like petals all along the bare branches. But note that all types of hamamelis must be given a neutral or acid soil, a sunny position (which they would obviously be given if planted near heaths), and a soil supplying a reasonable amount of moisture combined with good drainage. 'Pallida' will grow slowly to a height and spread of around 6ft (1.8m).

For February–March flowering one of the best-loved shrubs (of a size suitable for any garden) is the mezereon, *Daphne mezereum*, which produces its richly fragrant, purplish-red blooms thickly along the stems. It grows about 4ft (1.2m) tall and much the same wide, and its only fault is to occasionally decide that it has had enough and die off for no apparently good reason. For something so attractive the risk is worth taking. A well-drained soil is a necessity. *D. mezereum* is, of course, deciduous; an evergreen daphne which is of much the same size and decorative also at this time of year is *D. odora* 'Aureomarginata', this having pale green leaves margined with pale yellow and, in February and March, terminal heads of very fragrant, reddish-purple flowers. It is hardier than its slightly tender parent, *D. odora*, but it must be given a sheltered position.

One of the most valuable foliage shrubs for the garden in winter is *Elaeagnus pungens* 'Maculata', which quite slowly makes a bush up to 8ft (2.4m) tall and wide and which can, if necessary, be kept rather less than that by selective pruning. Its largish leaves are coloured a rich golden-yellow over a good part of their surface from the centre and bordered by dark green. Sometimes, branches will revert to pure green and these must be cut out. It has no special soil needs and will grow well on alkaline soils. Less well known is *E. pungens* 'Dicksonii', a slow-growing cultivar in which the yellow is carried in the outer part of the leaf rather than the inner. The slow rate of growth could be an advantage. For March–April flowering in the small garden I would strongly recommend *Magnolia stellata* and *Forsythia* 'Lynwood', the latter the best, I think, of its kind, with its rich yellow colouring, large flowers and the prodigality with which these are borne. Its dimensions are about 8ft by 8ft (2.4 x 2.4m). Forsythias are, of course, of the easiest cultivation, in sunshine or light shade. The star magnolia, *M. stellata*, is not a shrub for limy soils and it will do best on rather good loams which are moisture-retentive but well-drained. How delightful it is, though, with its shapely, rounded outline and spring burden of pure white flowers, each with many strap-shaped petals. It is much-branched and slow-growing but it can eventually make a bush some 10ft (3m) tall and wide.

If you have lime-free soil consider also some of the small rhododendrons like the 3ft (90cm) tall 'Tessa', which bears purplish pink, red-spotted flowers in March, and 'Seta', also March flowering, which has tubular pink flowers striped with a deeper shade of the same colour. This grows up to 5ft (1.5m) tall. As with all early-flowering rhododendrons, take care to keep them out of frost pockets or the blooms will be certain to suffer damage. Quite outstanding for April flowering is Elizabeth, which makes a spreading bush some 3 to 4ft (90cm–1.2m) tall, perfect for small gardens. Its very impressive trumpet-shaped blooms of bright scarlet are borne in trusses of up to five or six.

May sees the full flowering of the brooms, both *Genista* and *Cytisus* which share this common name. All need lashings of sunshine and light, well-drained soils in which to grow. A special favourite of mine is the dome-shaped Spanish gorse, *Genista hispanica*, a very prickly character indeed which literally smothers itself throughout May and early June with golden-yellow pea flowers. It grows about 3 to 4ft (90cm–1.2m) tall and more wide. If planted on a slight rise it looks marvellous with variously coloured sun roses (varieties of *Helianthemum nummularium*) around its base—in colours like orange, lemon-yellow, soft pink and bright yellow (even bright reds, if they are kept away from the bulk of the genista). A perfect choice for a bed on a retaining wall or for planting on a bank, where its arched branches can spill over, is the charming *Genista lydia*, which bears golden-yellow flowers from late May until late June. Only 2 to 3ft (60–90cm) tall, it has a spread of at least 6ft (1.8m).

Ideal for a raised bed is the procumbent *Cytisus kewensis*, no more than 1½ to 3ft (50–90cm) tall and with a spread of about 4 to 5ft (1.2–1.5m). This bears a mass of cream flowers in late April and May. I'm also very fond of the Warminster broom, *C. praecox*, larger at 5ft (1.5m) tall and wide, but very lovely indeed when smothered in cream flowers in May.

One of the most attractive variegated shrubs of medium size is undoubtedly *Weigela florida* 'Variegata', which bears pink foxglove-like flowers in May and June against a background of creamy white-edged leaves. The effect is cool and refreshing. It will usually make a bush 5 to 6ft (1.5–1.8m) tall and wide.

For flowering at the same time, another shrub not to be overlooked is the beautiful small Korean lilac named *Syringa velutina* (but still known to many as *S. palibiniana*), which does not usually grow over 5ft (1.5m) tall and wide and produces a wealth of small spikes of lilac-pink. Its leaves are small and roundish, of a fresh-looking light green. It should be given a home in a sunny position in well-drained soil.

The May- and June-flowering *Rhododendron yakushimanum* hybrids, so floriferous and attractive and compact of habit, are ideal for those small gardens where the soil is free of lime—and in gardens with alkaline soils they can, of course, be grown in containers, in lime-free compost (see p. 50). Naturally, there are variations in size and habit, but the average height of the considerable number now available is around 4ft (1.2m). Of special note are cultivars like the lavender 'Caroline Allbrook'; 'Percy Wiseman', with flowers of pink and cream which fade to creamy-white, with alluring effect; 'Dopey', a fine red; 'Hydon Hunter', with pink flowers rimmed at the petal edges with red and with orange spotting; and 'Morning Magic' in which pink buds open to blush-pink flowers which fade to white.

Two other genera which provide fine shrubs of modest size for early season flowering are *Escallonia* and *Philadelphus*. Of the escallonias—all of which grow well in any reasonable, well-drained soil, given a modicum of shelter—none is more calculated to please than 'Apple Blossom', which makes a bush some 4 to 5ft (1.2–1.5m) tall and wide and is in flower for months on end from early summer. As the name suggests, the blooms are a lovely shade of pink, merging to white low down on the petals. 'Glory of Donard', with carmine flowers, is another with a spread and height of about 5ft (1.5m).

The mock oranges (*Philadelphus*) have the great merit of doing well on thin, chalky soils as well as on any ordinary, well-drained soil. Sunshine or light shade is equally suitable. Varieties I would especially recommend include the creamy white, double-flowered 'Manteau d'Hermine', the white, single-flowered 'Avalanche', both up to 4ft (1.2m) tall and some 6ft (1.8m) wide, and 'Belle Etoile', another single with white, slightly maroon-blotched petals, which is several feet taller and wider.

Genista lydia, a superb dwarf shrub with a pendulous habit, may be kept more compact by light pruning immediately after flowering (see p. 29)

I'm very fond of *Senecio* 'Sunshine'. The spreading mound of grey foliage it provides is handsome in its own right, and it also makes an excellent foil for other plants of stronger colouring. In fact, the oval leaves are a soft green covered with a mass of grey hairs, as one sees when it is inspected close-to. Bright yellow daisy flowers are borne in quantity in late June and July, but it is as a foliage plant that it really excels itself. It requires a sunny position and a well-drained ordinary soil.

Euonymus fortunei 'Emerald an' Gold' is an excellent low-growing, foliage shrub. It is the colouring of the small, oval leaves which appeals so much: bright green and golden-yellow, with pinkish suffusions in the winter. It grows some 12 to 15 inches (30–37cm) tall and the plants should be spaced about 12 inches (30cm) apart to give thick cover. The variety 'Silver Queen' is of much the same height and has a spread of up to 3ft (90cm). Its leaves are margined with silvery white and these can also take on pink suffusions in winter. Against a wall it will climb to a height of 5 to 6ft (1.5–1.8m) and have a similar spread. These are suitable for sunny or lightly shaded positions.

The carpeting *Hebe pinguifolia* 'Pagei', with its dainty, glaucous bluish-grey leaves, is another useful plant. I grow it with the long-flowering *Geranium sanguineum lancastriense* 'Splendens', which has rose-pink flowers (the hebe is about 9 inches [22cm] tall, the geranium 12 inches [30cm]), for they complement each other very well. They should, of course, be planted in a sunny position.

I am very taken with the effectiveness of the compact-growing form of the deciduous *Physocarpus opulifolius* named 'Dart's Gold' as a summer-long foliage shrub of small size. A wealth of three- or five-lobed leaves, which start the season golden-yellow and only very slowly take on light green suffusions, are borne on a well-rounded bush some 2½ft (75cm) tall. White flowers are carried in June but these add little to its decorative value. Given the right companions in a mixed border, it can be extremely eye-catching. Its hardiness is not in doubt for it came through temperatures as low as 3°F (–16°C) in my garden in January 1986—with no adverse affect. It is happiest in moist but well-drained soil and needs exposure to sunshine to bring out the colour of the leaves.

On the face of it it sounds incongruous that a fine house plant should double-up as an excellent garden shrub of large proportions, but that is exactly what *Fatsia japonica* does—at least in warmer parts of the country, in reasonably sheltered positions. It can make a bush of spreading habit some 15ft (4.5m) tall and wide but it would be much more usual for it to settle down at about half that size. The palmate leaves—often as much as 15 or 16 inches (37–40cm) across—have up to nine lobes, a leathery texture and rich green colouring. It has very pronounced architectural merit. It is not at all surprising that it should also make a fine subject for a large container, but one thing which must be watched, if it is grown in that way, is its welfare in arctic weather conditions. The root system is more vulnerable and when such conditions threaten take the precaution of wrapping sacking or other protective material around the container.

Small gardens can often provide sunny, sheltered corners and that is just the kind of spot for the Jerusalem sage, *Phlomis fruticosa*, an evergreen with grey-green leaves up to 5 inches (12cm) long of sage-like appearance and distinctive bright yellow, stalkless and hooded flowers which are borne in whorls during the first half of summer. It has a rather sprawly habit and associates particularly well with paving, over which it can be allowed to extend. It grows to about 3 to 4ft (90cm–1.2m) tall and 5 to 6ft

(1.5–1.8m) wide. Its growth is rather soft, however, and it is liable to get cut back in winter.

For the length of their flowering (usually the summer through) and the ease of their cultivation, given a well-drained position, there is every reason to find space for potentillas, especially garden-raised hybrids like 'Primrose Beauty', pale primrose yellow in colour and some 4ft (1.2m) tall and 5ft (1.5m) wide: 'Klondyke', deep yellow, and a little smaller; and the rich yellow 'Elizabeth', which is lower-growing still and exceptionally long flowering. This is about 3ft (90cm) tall and up to 7 or 8ft (2.1–2.4m) wide. 'Red Ace' is the vermilion-red variety which caused such a stir some years ago by introducing a new colour to this flower. It can live up to its name but it can also be disappointing, for in wet weather and in very hot, dry weather the rich colour fades. The delightful 'Princess' has soft pink flowers which also tend to fade in hot, very dry spells. It grows some 2½ft (75cm) tall and wide.

No shrub of medium size is more deserving of a sunny place in the garden than the fine *Hypericum* 'Hidcote', which produces a profusion of large, saucer-shaped golden yellow flowers on a domed bush some 4ft (1.2m) high and 6ft (1.8m) wide from July into the autumn. It will do well in any reasonable, well-drained soil. From July also until September a bush of a lacecap hydrangea could be much appreciated for its attractive flowerheads—say the lovely *H. macrophylla* 'Bluewave' or 'Mariesii', both rose-pink or blue, depending on the soil type, or 'Whitewave' with pinkish centres and white, outer fertile flowers. These hydrangeas, like the ball-headed varieties, have their colouring determined by the pH of the soil, and thus on alkaline soils varieties which are normally blue become pink or red.

The hortensias I shall come to under plants for containers (see p. 52). Brief mention, however, of a variety of *H. serrata* which has blooms of globular shape, just like those of the hortensias but a little smaller. This is 'Preziosa' and its garden value is considerable, for these blooms are salmon-pink in colour, turning to a deeper shade as the season advances. With those go purple-tinged young foliage and stems. Its height is around 4 to 4½ft (1.3m) and it can be grown in sunshine or light shade, like all the hydrangeas. What must be avoided at all costs is subjecting them to dryness at the roots, especially in the growing season.

For late July and August flowering there is *Hydrangea paniculata* 'Grandiflora', which produces cone-shaped panicles of creamy-white flowers up to 18 inches (45cm) long. These become suffused with pink as they age. It can grow into a large bush with arched branches having a height of 10ft (3m) or more, but it can be kept much smaller by hard pruning in early spring, just before growth gets under way. This will result in fewer but larger flowers. It needs a good rich loam.

A delightful small shrub for September flowering is *Caryopteris* × *clandonensis* 'Arthur Simmonds' which produces tufty blue flowers on a grey-green-leaved bush some 3 to 4ft (90cm–1.2m) tall and wide. It will succeed in any well-drained soil in a sunny position but is liable to be cut back severely in hard winters. For this reason it is often necessary to hard prune it at the start of spring, which in any case leads to better flowers.

So far I have only mentioned one of the useful and easily pleased cotoneasters (*C. horizontalis*, see p. 24), but we come to them now as so many of them are at their best in the autumn. If you have a bank to cover there is nothing better for the purpose than the prostrate evergreen *C. dammeri*, which has a spread of as much as 9 or 10ft (2.7–3m) and smothers itself with brilliant red fruits in autumn. Another evergreen for the same purpose is *C. conspicuus* 'Decorus', which has a height of up to 3ft (90cm) and a spread of as much as 10ft (3m). They should preferably be given a sunny position, to ensure free-fruiting.

November is most definitely the month of *Mahonia* 'Charity', that superb evergreen shrub which opens its terminal racemes of rich yellow, fragrant flowers—borne up to 20 to a cluster and arching over in foot-long trails—against a background of truly spectacular leaves, each one of which is comprised of up to 21 spiny leaflets of dark green. It makes a large shrub, at least 8ft (2.4m) tall and 6ft (1.8m) wide (sometimes quite a lot more, but it can be pruned with care in spring). It grows well in any soil well supplied with moisture and well-drained, in sunshine or light shade. Flowering continues until late January.

For December I think it must be that old favourite, the evergreen laurustinus, *Viburnum tinus*, so valuable for its winter flowers, or rather its more compact form, 'Eve Price', which makes an attractive bush of 7 to 8ft (2–2.4m) tall and wide with smaller leaves than the parent plant, densely borne, and red buds which open to white, pink-tinged flowers. Against the dark green foliage, these flowers are a very handsome sight, and bloom throughout the winter. The excellent variety 'Gwenllian' makes a rather larger bush than 'Eve Price' and is usually free in producing blue berries which blend beautifully with the flowers.

Lastly, just a word about that other evergreen *Viburnum* species, *V. davidii*, which is attractive all the year round as low ground cover—it has a height of about 2ft (60cm) a spread of about 3ft (90cm)—with its narrowly oval, very dark green leaves, glossy and deeply veined, and (at times anyway) turquoise blue fruits if male specimens are planted with the female.

Making the most of roses

Roses deserve, and indeed were given early on, a handbook to themselves in this series, so my comments are restricted to brief mention of varieties which I believe have considerable potential in small gardens. Obviously, all the compact floribunda varieties are ideal, while climbing roses of all kinds must have a special role to play. Likewise the best of the modern bush roses (the large-flowered and cluster-flowered cultivars which we used to know as hybrid teas and floribundas), if their special qualities give them an edge over other contenders for valuable space. Shrub roses of the repeat-flowering kind? A few, where they, too, can make a real contribution; but not, alas, those old garden roses with one, all-too-brief, season of colour. And what about the miniatures, now gaining so much in popularity? These certainly do have a place in the small garden, especially for raised beds and for display near the home where their small stature can be an asset.

Clearly, the shorter cluster-flowered roses have an important part in the small garden; varieties, for instance, like the bright orange-scarlet 'Topsi' and creamy-white 'Bianco', which are only 1¼ft (38cm) tall, and excellent performers like the canary-yellow 'Kim', apricot-pink 'Peek-a-Boo' and light pink, white-eyed 'Regensberg', which are no more than 1½ft (45cm) tall. A little taller again, nearer 2ft (60cm), are the scarlet 'Trumpeter' and the yellow 'Bright Smile'. There are so many varieties in a wide colour range from which to make a choice.

A 3ft (90cm) tall cluster-flowered rose which looks delightful in association with paving is 'Yesterday', this carrying its small flowers in sprays which start off pink and fade to a lavender shade as they age—a charming combination. The foliage is small and thus in scale. The other rose which never looks better than in this kind of setting is 'Ballerina', a shrub rose with hybrid musk blood which makes a mass of growths to a height of 3 to 4ft (90cm–1.2m), is rather sprawly and delights the summer through with clusters of pale pink, white-eyed single blooms set among pale green foliage. 'Marjorie Fair' is a recent offspring from it, this having deep red flowers with a white eye. That old stager 'The Fairy' is another lovely variety, with soft peach, rosette-forming blooms carried over a very long period and attractive, glossy foliage. It grows some 3ft (90cm) tall and has a spreading habit.

Could there be a better large-flowered rose for a set-piece planting than 'Silver Jubilee'? With its beautiful, full blooms of pink, peach and cream and its good foliage, this is sure to be with us for many a year. Others of real distinction among the quite recently introduced cultivars are the deep yellow 'Freedom' and the highly fragrant, salmon-pink 'Paul Shirville', as well as the primrose-coloured 'Peaudouce'.

Of the numerous large-flowered climbers for growing on pillars—so suitable for giving height in the small garden while taking up little space—my choice would be 'Handel', a first-class variety with cream blooms flushed at the edges of the petals with rose-pink; multi-coloured 'Joseph's Coat', an amalgam of yellow, red and orange; 'Parkdirektor Riggers', brilliant scarlet; 'Pink Perpétue', clear pink with a carmine-pink reverse; and 'Compassion', a salmon-pink variety.

For the house walls, without question, it would be first of all the exquisite 'Climbing Cécile Brunner' and 'Phyllis Bide'. 'Climbing Cécile Brunner' is a glorious sight in early summer when smothering a large section of wall with its small, exquisitely shapely blooms of blush pink, and more flowers arrive during the rest of the summer although not in the quantities produced during the first flush. 'Phyllis Bide' usually grows to a height of about 7 or 8ft (2.1–2.4m) although it can go considerably higher, and this produces, against a. background of very attractive foliage, a succession of small, full-petalled, salmon-shaded, yellow flowers from early summer until deep into autumn. This much-neglected rose (raised in 1923) is deserving of far wider attention.

What a pity it is that that most beautiful of roses 'Mme Grégoire Staechelin' has such a relatively brief season of flowering, for its highly fragrant, large blooms, coral-pink shaded scarlet, make it one of the most desirable of all roses to have in the garden in June and July. This strong-growing, large-flowered climber, so stunning against a light coloured stone wall (it will do well with a north or east aspect) is still well worth giving space. Beauty and repeat-flowering go together in the splendid 'Mermaid', the *bracteata* climber which will climb to a height of 25ft (9m) or more and delight with its large, single blooms of pale yellow set off by a boss of amber stamens. This is a variety for a south- or west-facing wall, and not a rose for cold gardens.

Going back to the shrub roses, two that I would certainly want to fit in if at all possible would be, first, 'Golden Wings', a highly attractive fragrant variety of modest height (only 4ft [1.2m]) which bears large, single, pale yellow flowers with amber stamens throughout the summer. Then the much taller 'Fred Loads' with its brilliant vermilion-orange, single blooms. This grows to a height of 6 or 7ft (1.8–2.1m) and could give a real lift to a sunny corner of the garden.

The exquisite 'Phyllis Bide' (left), a fine rose for training against a wall, and 'Mme Grégoire Staechlin' (right), whose blooms are followed by large hips if not dead-headed

As to the miniatures, more and more of these seem to come along each year now, to join such excellent varieties as orange-red 'Starina'; red, striped white 'Stars 'n' Stripes'; pink 'Sweet Fairy'; and yellow and pink 'Baby Masquerade'. Newer cultivars include 'Dresden Doll', the pink miniature moss rose; yellow 'Rise 'n' Shine'; orange 'Hula Girl'; and coral-red 'Fashion Flame'. Raised beds, as I remarked earlier, and containers, are the natural homes for these.

Perennials for pleasure

Everyone who gardens for enjoyment knows the unending possibilities it offers as a leisure pursuit. What is not so often realised—for there is no reason why it should be given conscious thought—is the remarkable ability of gardening to evolve, with the passage of time; to stay in tune with changing life styles. The herbáceous perennials provide a perfect example of this, for, half a century ago, they were associated in the mind's eye with spacious, formal, herbaceous borders and with the organised confusion (if I may put it that way) of the cottage garden—with little in between. Now, in a word, they have been 'liberated', first through the development of the mixed border—of which there are such fine examples at Wisley—and then through the island-bed concept. It was Alan Bloom, the perennial plant specialist, who opened my eyes—as well as those of countless others—to the possibilities of this very large and fascinating group of plants.

Clearly, in the space at my disposal, I can only mention a limited number of these plants; but I have chosen them with care as being among the best, at least in my opinion, if the aim is to make maximum use of limited space. Two factors are of overriding importance when choosing perennials for the small garden: the quality of the plant (obviously) and the length of time during which it is likely to make a contribution to the garden. That doesn't mean that plants with rather short periods of display should be ruled out, but priority should be given to those which show up well in this respect.

Let us start with the hostas, which personify for me all that is best in perennials—a wide spread of interest, real quality and a large measure of adaptability, for although they are at their happiest in light shade, they are perfectly satisfactory in sunny positions provided they are well supplied with root moisture. But do concentrate on planting the most elegant of the species, varieties and hybrids. My favourite, without question, is one that grows to about 2ft (60cm), namely *H. crispula*—a joy from spring to autumn with its long, wavy-margined, sharp-pointed leaves of dark green, edged with white. Running a close second, however, is *H. undulata*, with pronounced undulation of the leaves as the name suggests, and a bold white sector irregularly margined with bright green. Both species bear lilac-coloured flowers in July and are roughly the same height. Outstanding also are the 2½ft (75cm) *H. fortunei* 'Albopicta', with leaves which start the season mainly rich yellow edged with green and which gradually change to primrose-yellow and green and then two shades of light and dark green; 'Thomas Hogg' in which the handsome leaves are broadly margined with cream; and 'Royal Standard' which carries its pure white flowers from August well into autumn above bold, fresh-green, heart-shaped leaves. The other two both have lilac-coloured blooms, those of 'Albopicta' arriving in mid-summer and those of 'Thomas Hogg' in early summer.

Two others I would mention are *H. lancifolia* and *H. tardiflora*. In both cases the name reflects the character of the plant. *Hosta lancifolia* has shiny, deep green, lance-shaped leaves and bears lilac flowers from July to September on 2ft (60cm) stems. *Hosta tardiflora* is only half that height, has shiny dark green leaves and bears lilac-mauve flowers in September and October. All hostas appreciate a good soil, with its ability to retain moisture while still remaining well-drained. This facility can be improved, of course, if necessary, by working in peat, garden compost, composted bark fibre or the like before planting, and mulching thereafter in spring with the same kind of materials.

If you believe, as I do, that yellow is a colour of which it is difficult to have too much in the garden, then allow me to suggest three quite different kinds of perennials which will provide this colour over a long period. First, a doronicum with its daisy-like blooms, the German-raised 'Spring Beauty' ('Frühlingspracht'), which produces a mass of showy, double flowers of rich yellow between late March and the end of May. As it has a height of only 1½ft (45cm) there are many spots in which this can be used, especially as it will do well in any reasonable soil in sunshine or light shade.

Next, that very reliable and free-flowering coreopsis, *C. verticillata* 'Grandiflora', also 1½ft (45cm) tall, which bears its golden-yellow daisy flowers above very thin, fern-like foliage from the beginning of July to the end of September. This must be exposed to plenty of sunshine. Then, to round off the season, the splendid cone-flower or black-eyed Susan, the 2½ft (75cm) tall *Rudbeckia fulgida* 'Goldsturm', another sun-lover, which associates beautifully with *Sedum* 'Autumn Joy' and *S. spectabile* varieties like 'Brilliant'. The overlap of flowering times occurs in September and October and the sedum would be planted in front with its height of about 1½ft (45cm). 'Goldsturm', with its bright yellow flowers so splendidly set off by the black central cones, is in flower from early July until September and often deep into October.

There is no perennial which gives better value for the space occupied than *Salvia nemorosa* 'Superba'. A bold clump of this 3ft

(90cm) tall plant is a fine sight. It throws up a thick mass of bluish-purple flower spikes in the July–September period and associates beautifully with numerous yellow-flowered plants, preferably with contrasting flower shapes. The similarly sized, flat-headed *Achillea* 'Coronation Gold' springs readily to mind, both having the same need for plenty of sunshine. Any reasonably good soil will suffice.

The herbaceous geraniums are first-rate garden plants. Consider *Geranium* 'Johnson's Blue', for example. This splendid plant produces a succession of light blue flowers on 1½ft (45cm) stems from May right through to September and has handsome, deeply cut foliage. Now *G. psilostemon* cannot match 'Johnson's Blue' for length of flowering, but it can for sheer beauty. Its deeply cut leaves are large and of mid-green colouring and it makes a bushy mound some 3ft (90cm) tall which forms a backdrop, in June and July, for the lovely magenta-crimson, black-centred flowers. In a word, it is superb.

Both of those just mentioned are excellent ground cover plants, like so many of their kind, in light shade or in sunny positions. I will confine my remarks to just two more, 'Claridge Druce' and *G. endressii* 'A. T. Johnson'. The first is a hybrid of real worth which makes thick clumps of deeply cut leaves and, in June and July, bears lilac-pink flowers. It is a first-class, 1½ft (45cm) tall ground-cover plant for sunshine or shade. *G. endressii* 'A. T. Johnson' is 1ft (30cm) tall, bears silvery pink flowers from June to September, and is also an admirable ground-cover plant.

Another genus which gives good value for the owner of a small garden is euphorbia, with the benefits coming in the spring and early summer months. The shade-tolerant and very showy *Euphorbia robbiae* is a good plant to have in the garden for it provides excellent ground cover, making a dense mat some 1½ft (45cm) tall with its rosettes of dark green leaves topped in May and June by yellow bracts. *Euphorbia griffithii* 'Fireglow' is another very useful plant, although taller (2½ft [75cm]) and at its decorative best in early summer, when it produces its orange-red flowers. This is better in sunshine but is perfectly satisfactory in shade. Likewise the 1½ft (45cm) tall *E. polychroma* (which used to be known as *E. epithymoides*), which is very distinctive in April and May with its bright yellowish green flowers. Again, they are good ground coverers.

Do try and find room, if you can, for *E. characias*, for this is a superb specimen plant some 4ft (1.2m) tall and wide which produces a mass of green, brown-centred blooms in large terminal heads in May and June. You can grow this in sunshine or light shade. None of these euphorbias has any soil fads.

The oriental poppies (varieties of *Papaver orientale*) tend to die down quite early in the summer and so, if you are not careful, leave ugly holes in the planting scheme of which they are part. But that problem can be easily overcome by siting them behind leafy, low-growing perennials. Their flowers are a joy as spring gives way to summer, whether they are those of orange-scarlet 'Marcus Perry'; 'Perry's White', white, with near black blotches; or maybe the delicately coloured salmon-pink 'Mrs Perry', which is the one I like best of all. In recent years, too, a spate of excellent new varieties has arrived, among them 'Picotee', salmon on a white ground and with frilly-edged petals; 'Harvest Moon', orange; and 'Black and White', white with black markings at the base of the petals. All are between 2½ and 3ft (70–90cm) tall and will grow in any ordinary, well-drained soil in a sunny position.

That brings me to the June-flowering herbaceous peonies—truly magnificent plants, which, quite apart from their flowers, contribute with their foliage to the appearance of the garden. It is often overlooked that the foliage colours most attractively in autumn, to soft browns, ochres and yellows. But, of course, it is the flowers which really matter. If I were to pick out a few of the

Paeonia 'Festiva Maxima' has large heavy blooms which may need staking (see p. 42)

double-flowered *Paeonia lactiflora* varieties, they would be deep rose-red 'Felix Crousse'; white, flecked reddish-purple 'Festiva Maxima'; apple-blossom pink 'Sarah Bernhardt'. Of the so-called Imperial varieties (single varieties with centres of petal-like staminodes), it would be the superb pink and creamy yellow 'Bowl of Beauty', 3ft (90cm) tall and a glorious sight in early summer. These will do well in sunshine or light shade in a nicely moist soil, but the more sunshine the better the flowering. If you want to grow something in the connoisseur class, however, it must be *P. mlokosewitschii*, a Caucasian species some 2½ft (70cm) tall which produces glorious cup-shaped blooms of pale yellow with a prominent centrepiece of golden yellow stamens in April against a background of pale green foliage.

I find the goat's beard, *Aruncus dioicus* (*A. sylvester*), an invaluable plant in early summer when it produces those marvellous plumes of creamy white flowers on stems 4 to 5ft (1.2–1.5m) tall. I grow it with cream-coloured shrub roses and mauve rhododendrons which also flower in June, but it is equally desirable with many other companions. It is best in the kind of light shade provided by a nearby canopy of high-branched trees. Again, plenty of soil moisture is desirable. If height is a problem there is a smaller version of it—the 2½ft (75cm) tall *A. dioicus* 'Kneiffii', which has similarly coloured flower plumes. Both have ferny-looking foliage which is an attraction until the end of the season.

The day lilies (or *Hemerocallis*) are popular for two very good reasons: they are easy to grow and, depending on variety, will provide a succession of colour with their lily-like flowers from early summer until September. That is not all, however, for the clumps of arched, grass-like leaves start the season a pale green which can be very attractive in spring, with this colour deepening as the weeks pass to a strong green. In autumn the leaves turn to yellow in their dying days. Orange, reds, pinks and yellows are the flower colours available, and new varieties of merit are coming along all the time. Established varieties to look out for especially are the small-flowered 'Golden Chimes', a fine deep yellow; rich crimson 'Stafford'; and primrose-coloured 'Whichford', with greenish centres to the flowers. Mostly these are 2½ to 3ft (70–90cm) tall, but some fall outside this range and notably the new 'Stella d' Oro', with orange-throated, canary yellow flowers, which is only 1¾ft (53cm) tall.

Don't rule out the tall bearded irises even though they provide only a few weeks of colour in May–June. Just a few carefully chosen varieties can be well worth while, if one allows that the sword-like foliage makes a splendid foil for other plants of different habit. These, of course, need plenty of sunshine and well-drained soil—don't make the mistake of planting the rhizomes too deeply; these should have their tops level with the soil surface. Excellent varieties include the pale blue 'Jane Phillips', yellow and chestnut red 'Staten Island' and 'Berkeley Gold', golden yellow.

The iris tribe generally is fascinating, but the only other ones which I shall mention here are the variegated forms of *I. pallida* and *I. foetidissima*. The first, for planting in a sunny position in well-drained soil, is available in two forms, one having white longitudinal stripes on the grey-green, sword-like leaves, the other yellow stripes. Of the two I find the white the more compelling in the garden, but both are excellent plants some 2 to 3ft (60–90cm) tall which can have a dramatic impact if several are planted together. These bear lavender-coloured flowers which are of less importance than the foliage.

The Gladwyn iris, *I. foetidissima*, is, of course, a good plant for shade and is very handsome indeed when the seed pods split open revealing the scarlet seeds. Its form 'Variegata' has cream longitudinal leaf variegation and is another desirable plant to help bring character to a mixed planting.

While on the subject of variegation, don't overlook the charms of the low-growing ground-coverer named *Brunnera macrophylla* 'Variegata' which has heart-shaped leaves heavily marked with cream and, in April, bright blue, forget-me-not-like flowers borne in tiny sprays. It is a good plant for light shade and nicely moist soil—soil and conditions which well suit the pulmonarias or lungworts (which also have very interesting, mottled foliage). One of the best is the foot-high (30cm) *Pulmonaria saccharata* 'Pink Dawn', which flowers from March to May and has funnel-shaped blooms of rose-pink complemented most attractively by the white-mottled foliage.

Similar conditions to the above would be just right also for the willow gentian, *Gentiana asclepiadea*, a delight between July and September when it bears, on arched 2½ft (75cm) long stems, rich blue, narrowly funnel-shaped flowers against a background of willow-like leaves. It is a lovely plant and there is a fine variety named 'Knightshayes' which has flowers of deeper colour than the parent.

What cheerfulness the crocosmias bring to the garden in the second half of summer, especially the species *Crocosmia masonorum* and its outstanding form 'Firebird'. These carry from late July to September arching sprays of orange flowers above the sword-like foliage, which is typical of crocosmias generally and makes such an effective foil for the blooms. Its height is about 2½ft

(75cm). Somewhat taller (a little over 3ft [90cm]) is the hybrid 'Lucifer', with *Curtonus paniculatus* on one side of its parentage and crocosmia on the other (these genera are closely related). This comparative newcomer is a superb plant with arching sprays of brilliant red flowers borne in July and August, or from late June in some gardens. It has good foliage and has proved to be a very strong-growing plant. In flower, it makes a great impact. The flowers are also excellent for cutting for the home.

Culturally, the crocosmias are easy plants to please, growing well in any soil of average quality which is well drained but nicely retentive of moisture. They grow from corms and should rightly be placed with the bulbous plants in this book, but among the perennials they find their natural home. They are best grown in sunny, sheltered positions. They are clump-forming and spread quickly and lifting and division is usually necessary every third or fourth year to maintain quality. This is best done in early spring but can be done in early autumn.

Space runs short but there are a few other plants which simply must be included. *Polygonum bistorta* 'Superbum', for instance, $2\frac{1}{2}$ to 3ft (75–90cm) tall and a wonderful sight when its pink poker-like blooms are borne above the tumbling mass of rather coarse leaves between May and July. It will grow well in sunshine or light shade and in a sunny position is ideal for mixing with the lighter-coloured brooms—those with cream flowers like *Cytisus praecox*. It must have an adequate supply of root moisture, but otherwise its needs are few. Another plant which always attracts attention when it is in bloom is *Stachys macrantha* 'Superba'. It makes a ground-covering mat of dark green leaves with attractively wrinkled surfaces above which are borne in June and July whorls of rosy-mauve, hooded flowers on $1\frac{1}{2}$ to 2ft (45–60cm) stems. It flowers best in a sunny position but is satisfactory, too, in light shade.

Then there is that outstanding aster, *A.* × *frikartii*, which bears a mass of lavender blue, daisy-like flowers with orange centres from July to September—this makes a marvellous companion for *Rudbeckia fulgida* 'Goldsturm' which I mentioned earlier (see p. 39). And, of course, in a different category again, the perennial adored by all flower arranging ladies: *Alchemilla mollis*, the lady's mantle, with its roundish, scalloped, pale green leaves and dainty sprays of greenish yellow flowers throughout most of the summer. It will grow equally well in sunshine or shade.

Getting towards the end of the year, you should be aware of the value of *Schizostylis coccinea* (preferably in its form 'Major'), which bears racemes of bright red star-shaped flowers above sword-like leaves from late September to November. There are two excellent pink-flowered varieties, 'Viscountess Byng' and 'Mrs Hegarty'. In all but favoured gardens they must be given a sunny, sheltered position in a wall bed, and they must be grown in soil which retains plenty of moisture in the growing season. The rhizomes should be protected in winter by giving them a covering of dry litter.

A plant which is little known and very useful for late colour—and as a useful ground cover—is *Liriope muscari*. This has grassy, evergreen leaves of dark green and produces from August to November spikes of grape-hyacinth-like blooms of violet-purple on stems 1ft (30cm) tall. You can grow it in any ordinary soil in sunshine or light shade.

By the end of the year we can enjoy the beautiful flowers of the Algerian iris, *Iris unguicularis* (still often known as *I. stylosa*). These flowers may be anything from pale lavender-blue to something approaching purple in colour. It must be given a home in full sun (so that the rhizomes will get thoroughly baked in summer), sheltered from the elements and in a poorish but impeccably well-drained soil.

The hellebores are invaluable, from the Christmas rose, *Helleborus niger*, which again needs a nicely sheltered home, preferably in a bed against a north-facing wall if this is not exposed to cold winds (for this plant must not be allowed to dry out in hot sunshine in summer) to the Lenten roses (varieties of *H. orientalis*). Then there is the pale-green-flowered stinking hellebore, *H. foetidus*, with its handsome much segmented foliage; and, the finest of them all, the Corsican hellebore, *H. corsicus*, with its large heads of cup-shaped, pale green flowers and very handsome leaves.

Some gardeners take a rather superior attitude towards the bergenias, describing the leaves, for instance, as 'cabbagey'. They are first-rate plants, make magnificent ground cover with their evergreen foliage and are very pleasing in flower with the various species, varieties and hybrids providing welcome colour from March (or even earlier) to May. My favourites are the 1 to 1½ft (30–45cm) tall 'Ballawley' with rose-red flowers in March and April and leaves which become suffused with bronzy-red in winter; pure white 'Silberlicht' ('Silver Light'), 1ft (30cm) tall and April–May flowering; and *B. × schmidtii* which has especially attractive, bright green leaves and pale pink flowers from the beginning of March or even earlier until April. *Bergenia cordifolia* 'Purpurea' is the variety most frequently encountered, this having rounded leaves (which take on purplish overtones in winter) and purplish pink flowers in bold heads in March and April. It is an excellent plant.

A selection of bulbous flowers

With such a wide field to cover in very little space, I must be highly selective in my treatment of this important sector of the plant world. I shall begin with the daffodils or narcissi for many gardeners would, perhaps, consider them a priority. The most important group within this huge genus is, in my opinion, the *cyclamineus* hybrids, obtained by crossing this beautiful little daffodil with trumpet varieties to give a selection of varieties in the 8 inch to 15 inches (20–38cm) height range. These are perfectly suited for planting in beds and borders, around the base of deciduous shrubs, for instance, and for growing in containers or in raised beds, where perhaps they can be enjoyed from the house windows. Some of the best are 'February Gold', 12 inches (30cm) tall, quite often able to live up to its name and usually in flower by early March; golden yellow 'Peeping Tom', of much the same size and early-flowering; 'March Sunshine', 15 inches (38cm), bright yellow with a golden trumpet and March flowering; and 'Jack Snipe', 8 inch (20cm), creamy white with a yellow cup and flowering in late March and early April.

Narcissus cyclamineus itself is only 5 inches (12cm) tall, deep yellow in colour, and with a long, narrow trumpet with swept-back petals at its base—very beautiful indeed. If you want to grow it or other dwarf species like the hoop petticoat daffodil, *N. bulbocodium*, then choose a sheltered spot where the soil is especially well-drained, and plant them 3 inches (8cm) deep. The larger kinds, like the hybrids just mentioned, need planting at a depth of 4 inches (11cm).

If the narcissi are a first love for so many of us, the snowdrops (or *Galanthus*) must run them a close second. On a cold January day it is a welcome sight to find that the first *Galanthus nivalis* plants are in bloom. One of the finest of the *nivalis* varieties is 'S. Arnott', rather bigger and stronger growing than the parent and a lovely sight with its white flowers marked with a little green on their inner segments. This grows about 8 inches (20cm) tall. For later flowering there is the so-called giant snowdrop, *Galanthus elwesii*, from western Turkey and certain Greek islands in the Aegean Sea. This has globular white flowers boldly marked with green on the inner segments and broad, glaucous leaves. Snowdrops grow well in sunshine or light shade, but like plenty of moisture in the soil. It is also more satisfactory to obtain growing plants in the spring (which are available from some suppliers) than to plant dry bulbs in the autumn.

Equally accommodating are the *Muscari* (or grape hyacinths) which also do well in sunny positions in any ordinary, well-drained soil. So are the scillas, which are so delightful to have growing in small beds flanked by paving, in raised beds and so on. There is nothing more pleasant than to be able to enjoy in March the brilliant blue of the flowers of a variety like *Scilla sibirica* 'Atro-purpurea' (or 'Spring Beauty' as it is also called). The most popular of all muscari, understandably, is *Muscari armeniacum* 'Heavenly Blue'.

For sunny positions in the garden there are a great many *Crocus chrysanthus* varieties for February–March flowering; likewise the larger-flowered Dutch varieties. But none of these, in my opinion, have the charms of *Crocus tommasinianus* and its violet purple variety 'Whitewell Purple'. These are incredibly good colonisers and look delightful around the base of a conifer or making themselves at home in a border. *C. tommasinianus* itself has mauve-blue flowers borne on 3 inch (8cm) tall stems and is always in flower by February.

For shade, one should consider the winter aconite, *Eranthis hyemalis*, for this will naturalise itself in shrub and other borders and bring a welcome splash of strong yellow to the scene in February and March—indeed, even in January in the most congenial of climatic conditions.

The snowflakes, leucojums, should certainly not be left out of the reckoning for they are highly decorative plants, with the early-flowering *Leucojum vernum* making its display in February and March and the so-called summer snowflake, *L. aestivum*, flowering in April and May. Both like to be grown in well-drained but moderately moisture-retentive soil and, while successful in both sunshine and light shade, are probably happiest in the latter. The bulbs should be planted in late August or September, as soon as they can be obtained.

The 6 inch (15cm) tall *L. vernum* produces its white, green-tipped flowers above a wealth of broadly strap-shaped, rather thick and dark green leaves. The flowers are reminiscent of those of the snowdrop but differ in that in this case all the petals are of equal length (the inner ones are shorter in the snowdrops). Not too easy to come across but highly desirable is the variety *carpathicum* in which the petals are tipped with yellow.

The summer snowflake, *L. aestivum*, grows to a height of about 2ft (60cm) and naturalises freely. It makes a good plant, therefore, to grow near the front of borders in association with herbaceous perennials and shrubs, when it will soon make a real contribution. White, bell-shaped flowers are borne in terminal umbels in pendant array. Again, the petals are green tipped. The leaves are strap-shaped, up to 18 inches (50cm) in length and bright green in colour. 'Gravetye Giant', which there is no difficulty in obtaining, is a fine form of the species.

So far as the tulips are concerned, I shall confine my comments on the bedders to just two types: the splendid Darwin hybrids, some 2ft (60cm) tall, which carry their spectacular blooms in late April and early May, and the wonderfully elegant lily-flowered varieties which also come into bloom in early May. For set-piece plantings the varieties belonging to these two types are unsurpassed. However, in the small garden the ones which should be considered more closely are the superb *Tulipa kaufmanniana* hybrids (which have arisen from crossing this species with *T. greigii*), the *fosteriana* and the *greigii* hybrids. The *kaufmanniana* varieties are so called water-lily tulips in popular parlance, and very lovely they are with their fine flowers and, mostly, handsomely striped foliage. Most fall in the 4 to 8 inch (10–20cm) height range which makes them ideal for growing in raised beds, the forefront of borders, among rock garden plants and in containers. They are in flower in March and April. Excellent varieties include the yellow and red 'Stresa'; 'Heart's Delight', a mixture of pale rose, golden-yellow and ivory-white; and 'Shakespeare', salmon, apricot and orange.

The *fosteriana* hybrids, mostly from 8 to 15 inches (20–38cm) in height, are in flower from early April and by far the best known of these is the magnificent 'Madame Lefeber' (also known as 'Red Emperor'), which bears large scarlet flowers marked with black at their base. The fosterianas are followed into flower in mid April by the *greigii* hybrids. These have a height range of 8 to 16 inches (20–40cm) and the star of these is undoubtedly the scarlet 'Red Riding Hood', 8 inches (20cm) tall and with the most lovely mottled and striped foliage (a characteristic of the type). Try these interplanted with muscari and you will find the effect delightful. Two other *greigii* hybrids of great charm are 'Plaisir', an amalgam of carmine red and shades of yellow to near white, and 'Toronto', a very distinctive rosy coral shade with yellow markings near the base of the flower.

Our native snake's head fritillary, *Fritillaria meleagris*, is a delight in April whether grown in borders or in grass, where it will usually naturalise freely. What intrigues is the soft colouring and chequerboard markings of the pendent bell-shaped flowers, which vary in colour from purple to reddish- and violet-purple and white. Named varieties are available and selected mixed strains. Plant the bulbs up to 6 inches (15cm) deep in autumn in soil which remains nicely moist but well-drained.

The other popular fritillary for garden planting is *F. imperialis*, the crown imperial. It is a most distinctive and beautiful plant with its wealth of bold foliage clothing the lower part of the 4ft (1.2m) stems and, as the *pièce de résistance*, the topknot of small leaves under which hang the large, bell-shaped flowers, ranging in colour from orange and orangey-brown to orange-red, brick red and shades of yellow from deep hues to lemon, depending on the variety in question. Two of the widely available varieties are 'Lutea Maxima', golden-yellow, and 'Rubra', orange-red. Plant the bulbs of crown imperials in early autumn in good, well-drained, but reasonably moisture-retentive soil in sunny positions.

Among the summer-flowering bulbs, the large-flowered gladiolus hybrids can be an important element in garden display, while the 2 to 3ft (60–90cm) tall, very pretty Primulinus hybrids and the 3 to 4ft (90cm–1.2m) tall Butterfly hybrids are superb for cutting for room decoration. The large-flowered varieties are so numerous that it is best to consult a catalogue regarding the choice one wishes to make. They need a good, moisture-retentive soil in a sunny sheltered part of the garden. Plant the corms in succession between late March and mid-May to spread out as much as possible the flowering times.

A sadly neglected summer-flowering bulbous plant of considerable charm is *Galtonia candicans*, a member of the lily family (*Liliaceae*) known as the summer hyacinth. It is indeed a member of the hyacinth tribe and was formerly known as *Hyacinthus candicans*, resembling a giant hyacinth—it is some 4ft (1.2m) tall—with pendent white bell flowers borne in loose racemes above glaucous, strap-shaped leaves. These flowers are displayed from July to September and are an asset to a mixed plant border at that time. Plant the bulbs some 5 to 6 inches (15cm) deep in a sunny position in spring and leave the plants undisturbed for as long as possible afterwards.

Space precludes me from saying much about the lilies, but *Lilium regale* is a superb, easily grown species. The white, trumpet-shaped blooms, marked with yellow in the throat and rosy-purple on the outside, are boldly borne on stems of 5 to 6ft (1.5–1.8m) in height. The flowering time is July. Of the many hybrids I would give pride of place to the Mid-Century Hybrids and especially the varieties 'Enchantment', nasturtium red and about 3ft (90cm) tall; lemon-yellow 'Destiny', which is just a little taller and is embellished with brown spots on the petals; and $2\frac{1}{2}$ft (75cm) tall 'Paprika', a fine deep red.

49

Tubs, pots and window-boxes

There is nothing new about growing plants in containers for outdoor decoration. It has been going on for centuries. What is new is the breadth of the interest in this kind of gardening, and the importance it has assumed. And that interest is, of course, directly related, first, to the decreasing size of gardens, and, secondly, to the very agreeable concept of treating a small garden as an outdoor room. Container-grown plants, which can be so enormously attractive, heighten that particular illusion.

Let us consider the use of plant containers in garden settings. Cost must enter into the equation and some of the most attractive containers can be pretty expensive, but that notwithstanding it would always be my advice to buy fewer and better rather than the reverse. Containers are available, of course, in a diversity of materials from hardwoods and reconstituted stone to asbestos-cement, glass-fibre and plastic. So, within the limitations of your pocket, match the containers to the setting and, equally important, to the plants which you intend to grow in them.

It is useless, on a practical level, to consider growing shrubs in containers which lack sufficient depth, for in no time at all the compost is exhausted and the roots of the plants unduly restricted. You must make sure, too, that the containers used have adequate provision made for the draining away of excess water, as regards drainage holes in their base and ground clearance. If necessary, support the container on bricks or blocks of some kind.

Again, it is essential to use good compost (indeed vital with permanent plants) if good results are to be achieved. Garden soil isn't up to the job. Either make up your own compost from good fibrous loam, peat and sharp sand or, more conveniently, use John Innes compost in one of its three grades or choose from the range of proprietary soilless composts. Excellent as the last-mentioned are for so many purposes, plants grown in these need regular feeding and even more careful attention to watering, while the anchorage provided for the roots of shrubs with plenty of top growth is not so effective as with soil-based compost. If you decide on John Innes compost, then the No. 1 grade would be right for short-term plants, No. 2 for semi-permanent plants and No. 3 for those which are going to stay put for a long time.

A few other reminders. If you are intending to grow lime-hating plants, be sure to obtain a lime-free growing medium for them. To prevent clogging of the drainage holes in the base cover these

Tuberous begonias, geraniums and fuchsias are ideal container plants

with a layer of crocks (not too readily available these days) or small stones and cover these in turn with roughage such as coarse peat. With permanent plantings of shrubs, annual top-dressing will give them a real boost. Remove the top $\frac{1}{2}$ to 2 inches (1.3–5cm) of compost just as growth is about to start in spring and replace this with fresh compost of the same type. But be very careful not to damage the roots while doing this. With all composts feeding will be necessary at some stage during the growing season. When and how much will depend on the type of compost and the plants being grown. It must always be remembered that, compared with growing in the open garden, this is a very artificial life for permanent plants. So which plants should be grown in this way? It must, of course, depend on the kind of garden you have, but the usual thing would be to have some permanent plants in containers but a much higher proportion of a transient nature—bulbs to start off the season and superb bedders like the *Begonia semper-virens* varieties and strains, petunias and marigolds to follow on.

In fact, a very large number of shrubs are well-suited for

51

container display. There is a rich choice to be had from the camellias and rhododendrons (which must be given lime-free compost in which to grow), and especially from the former as their foliage is such an attraction all the year round (see pp. 22–3).

Many rhododendrons and azaleas make admirable tub plants. Those I would especially recommend are the small-growing rhododendrons such as 'Praecox', 'Seta' and 'Pink Pebble', which bears its pale pink bell flowers in May. Also May-flowering and quite exquisite is *R. yakushimanum*, a Japanese species which makes a compact, rounded bush some 3 to 4ft (90cm–1.2m) tall which bears a profusion of white bell flowers opening from pink buds. Its handsome, lanceolate leaves are felted light brown on the underside. It is slow growing. Also, as I remarked on p. 30, you have a rich choice of *R. yakushimanum* hybrids to grow in this way, all with compact habits, fine flower trusses and attractive foliage. Of the azaleas, it is the evergreen kinds which have most to offer, and of these varieties like 'Vuyk's Rosy Red', the pure white, green-eyed 'Palestrina' and 'Rosebud', rose-pink, are some to be considered.

The value of fuchsias and hydrangeas (*Hydrangea macrophylla* varieties) for this purpose needs no underlining. Both are superb, the mop-headed hortensia hydrangeas in particular, and, in the case of fuchsias, the so-called hardy varieties which you can find offered in so many tree and shrub catalogues—varieties like scarlet and purple 'Mrs Popple' and the cerise and mauve 'Tom Thumb'. At the end of the season over-winter the plants in a frost-free greenhouse, shed or garage. For providing colour from mid-summer into autumn they are unexcelled.

And what else in shrubs? I especially recommend the evergreen *Fatsia japonica* for its architectural qualities (this you will find described on p. 32), and the Japanese maples (varieties of *Acer palmatum*) which, although deciduous, have a great deal to offer in the way of beautiful foliage and shapeliness. *Choisya ternata*, which I've already discussed on p. 22, is a joy in spring when bearing its fragrant blooms. For low plantings the evergreen *Euonymus japonicus* 'Microphyllus Variegatus' is a splendid foliage plant (it has white-margined leaves) to mix in with flowering plants, and you should not overlook the very real decorative value of that splendid dwarf cherry laurel, *Prunus laurocerasus* 'Otto Luyken' which makes a bush some 3 to 4ft (90cm–1.2m) tall and somewhat more in width. This has rather small, narrow, dark green leaves with a shiny surface and it is handsome the year round. White flowers are borne in spikes in May. Among decorative foliage evergreen shrubs is *Elaeagnus × ebbingei* 'Gilt Edge', in which the large leaves are

Varieties of *Phormium tenax* and *P. cookianum*, striking foliage plants but not reliably hardy

irregularly margined with golden yellow—ideal for bringing a splash of colour to a part of the garden difficult to liven up in other ways. And do not forget the slow-growing *Elaeagnus pungens* 'Dicksonii', which has yellow-splashed leaves (see p. 28).

As specimen plants for tubs, standard or half-standard bay laurels are always attractive. This evergreen, *Laurus nobilis*, must be given a sunny, sheltered position, otherwise the dark, glossy green leaves (which are aromatic) may be damaged by frost or cold winds. It is especially vulnerable while young.

Clematises and climbing roses in variety can be used as tub plants with stunning effect. So can the Russian vine, *Polygonum baldschuanicum*, the Virginia creeper, *Parthenocissus quinquefolia*, *Hedera colchica* 'Dentata Variegata' and *H. helix* varieties, all of which are described in the chapter on climbing and wall plants.

Of special interest are the varieties of *Phormium* (ornamental flax) which have been introduced from New Zealand in the past few years. These are mostly derived from the New Zealand flax, *Phormium tenax*, a few from the smaller-growing (4ft [1.2m] tall) *P. cookianum*. Both species have been grown in Britain for a very long time, *tenax*, indeed, for almost 200 years. As foliage plants with architectural merit these new varieties have plenty to offer with their duo- or multi-toned, evergreen, sword-like foliage and interesting shapes. They include 'Dazzler', 2 to 2½ft (60–75cm) tall with a reddish brown ground colour blended longitudinally with carmine-red; 'Yellow Wave', similarly sized, golden yellow edged with green; 'Sundowner', greyish purple broadly margined with pink-suffused cream; and 'Tricolor' (a *cookianum* variety) which is a striking combination of green and white stripes margined with red. But a word of caution: these plants are susceptible to damage in severe weather conditions, which is why there is a distinct advantage in growing them in containers rather than in beds (for which they are perfectly suitable, given winter protection with dry litter around the base). Grown in containers, they can so easily be kept over winter in a frost-proof place (which needs to be well lit) until they go outdoors again in about May.

Small-growing conifers certainly have their uses as 'pot plants', especially the popular *Chamaecyparis lawsoniana* 'Ellwoodii', grey-green-foliaged and columnar, and 'Ellwood's Gold', a sport of it which has yellow-tipped leaves (the slow growth of this variety could be an advantage). Another chamaecyparis which is widely available is *C. pisifera* 'Boulevard', conical in outline, and thickly furnished with silvery-blue foliage which takes on almost purplish suffusions in winter. Then there is *Juniperus media* 'Mint Julep', with lovely, splayed-out wispy growth of bright green colouring, and *J. media* 'Blaauw' which has upward-thrusting branches of bluish grey which arch over at the tips. There are many more suitable conifers on which the enterprising gardener can call for this kind of display, including most of those mentioned on pp. 15–17. (See also the Wisley handbook on conifers.)

Among bedding plants (see also pp. 56–60), my front-runners for this kind of display would be the fibrous-rooted *Begonia semperflorens* varieties and strains, the petunias and marigolds and the delightfully colourful forms of *Phlox drummondii*. There are also the geraniums (pelargoniums), now so readily raised from seed (early in the year, under glass, in heat); dwarf antirrhinums and dwarf verbenas, varieties of *Salvia splendens* and ageratums. All of these can be grown in containers as restricted in size as window-boxes.

An extremely wide range of bulbs is suitable for growing in window-boxes and other containers (see pp. 46–9 for suggestions). You can, of course, also use some window-box space to grow herbs like mint, thyme, chives and parsley.

On a purely practical note, do make sure that any window-boxes you have are very firmly secured. The containers and compost can be extremely heavy. Be assiduous in your attention to watering, especially during hot weather. Containers of all kinds can dry out with surprising rapidity, and hanging baskets most of all. These can sometimes need attention several times a day—but don't be discouraged by that for the rewards are great.

Raised beds

Raised beds have really come into their own in recent years as an aid to the handicapped and the elderly. But such beds have an application in a great many gardens purely as a design feature which will allow small plants, from alpines and rock plants generally to small bulbous flowers and even shrubs and perennials tending towards the miniature, to be displayed to maximum advantage.

Such a feature will, in the nature of things, have impeccable drainage, and that is something so many plants enjoy. The bulbous flowers I have mentioned, the smallest of slow-growing conifers, miniature roses and miniature shrubs like the creeping willow, *Salix uva-ursi*, or the golden-yellow stemmed *Hebe armstrongii*, which has closely adpressed leaves of yellowish green (now correctly known as *H. ochracea*), are all suitable candidates.

Raised beds come in for full consideration in Will Ingwersen's *Alpines Without a Rock Garden* in this series. If you are interested in having such a feature without specialising then I would suggest a visit to Wisley to see the beds there.

A raised bed planted with tulips, wallflowers and forget-me-nots

Colour from annuals and biennials

Hardy annuals first, because minimal facilities are needed to grow these to perfection. Perhaps two of the most significant hardy annuals to be introduced in recent years are the mallows, *Lavatera* 'Silver Cup' and 'Mont Blanc'. These are very impressive plants indeed, making bushy specimens which literally smother themselves with bold trumpet flowers from July to September from seeds sown direct in the border in spring. To obtain plants which will come into flower earlier, seeds can be sown under glass in March with the resulting plants being set out in May. 'Silver Cup' is rose-pink in colour, with streaks of deeper pink on the petals, and 2½ft (75cm) tall; 'Mont Blanc', as the name suggests, is dazzling white and grows to 2ft (60cm) tall.

Sweet peas are almost everybody's favourite, and it would be difficult to overestimate the importance of developments like the splendid Jet Set Mixed strain, which provides such fine-quality flowers on plants only 3ft (90cm) tall. For the small garden particularly they are a delight, both for garden display (perhaps grown as a low hedge between two parts of the garden) and for cutting. Likewise, the slightly smaller Little Elfin Mixed strain. Then there is the Patio strain which is only 1ft (30cm) tall. This is ideal for confined quarters, and for growing in containers.

Nasturtiums are, of course, invaluable for providing bright colour, and of these the dwarf Jewel strain with its excellent colour range is ideal for growing in containers. For this last use, too, keep *Convolvulus* 'Blue Flash' in mind. This is a striking plant with its mass of rich blue, white and yellow-centred blooms.

The lovely little Californian poppies, or eschscholzias, are easy to grow well in sunny positions (like the nasturtiums and convolvulus just mentioned). Good mixtures include Monarch Art shades and the very pretty Ballerina mixture in which the flower petals are fluted. All come in a good range of colours.

Then there are the godetias of which the best, I think most of us would agree, is the exquisite 'Sybil Sherwood', 15 inches (38cm) tall. It belongs to the azalea-flowered section and bears salmon-pink blooms edged with white, in abundance, over a very long period in summer. A perfect companion for it is the straw-coloured 1 to 1½ft (30–45cm) tall squirrel-tail grass, *Hordeum jubatum*, also annual and available from some seed firms. And while on the subject of grasses, don't overlook the charms of the pearl grass, *Briza maxima* (often called quaking grass, which is a name applied to the brizas generally); this grows about 15 inches (38cm) tall and is a very elegant sight indeed with its mass of pendent spikelets nodding in the slightest breeze.

One of the loveliest annuals, in my opinion, is *Limnanthes douglasii*, a Californian native, which was long ago dubbed the poached egg flower here (from the appearance of the white, yellow-centred flowers). Give it a sunny position and it is very easily pleased. Cornflowers (*Centaurea cyanus* varieties), annual poppies (forms of *Papaver rhoeas*, like the Shirley Single Mixed strain) and love-in-the-mist (*Nigella damascena* varieties like 'Miss Jekyll' and the Persian Jewels strain) can all give a great deal of pleasure.

The half-hardy kind, of course, are a little more trouble to raise for they cannot be planted out until late May or early June, after proper hardening-off. Of these, the most significant in my reckoning are the forms of *Begonia semperflorens*; the petunias; forms of *Phlox drummondii*; the rudbeckias 'Marmalade', and 'Rustic Dwarfs' and the double and semi-double flowered 'Goldilocks'; tobacco plants (*Nicotiana*); marigolds (*Tagetes*) of various kinds; and dahlias like the single-flowered Dandy strain and the semi-double 'Redskin'.

The fibrous-rooted *Begonia semperflorens* varieties and strains are available in almost bewildering quantity. My favourites are the compact-growing Organdy mixture of some 8 inches (20cm) in height, an excellent range of colours from red and pink to white and green and bronze-foliaged plants, and the taller (1ft [30cm]) 'Danica Red' and 'Danica Rose'. These begonias and others of their kind continue flowering well into the autumn and if you lift some plants then, pot them up and bring them indoors when they will continue to produce blooms deep into winter. Marvellous value! So too are the Nonstop strain of tuberous-rooted begonia. The colour range is excellent, the flowers are double and the name Nonstop is an accurate portrayal of their garden performance. These can be grown from seed, which is why they are mentioned here, or tubers can be purchased.

Of the petunias the Resisto strain does, as claimed, stand up especially well to bad weather. Again, these come in a delightful range of colours and in dwarf versions a few inches shorter than the rest at 1ft (30cm) tall. Turning to *Phlox drummondii*, my choice would be Beauty Mixed, 15 inches (38cm) tall and with large flowers in a good range of colours, and the Carnival mixture which is slightly shorter.

Rudbeckia 'Marmalade' and 'Rustic Dwarfs' are superb garden plants, and excellent for cutting into the bargain. 'Marmalade' has golden-yellow ray flowers with bold black discs; 'Rustic Dwarfs', again with black discs, is a mixture of bronze, mahogany-red and yellow. The double and semi-double flowered 'Goldilocks' is the most recent to be introduced, the colour golden yellow. All are around 2ft (60cm) tall. Although they are very much plants for sunny positions, they stand up remarkably well to adverse weather, especially the first two. These can be given the usual half-hardy treatment (sowing in heat between February and April) or can be treated as biennials.

Earlier on I mentioned the nicotianas, or tobacco plants. A delightful strain to use to fill pockets in a mixed planting is the 2 to $2\frac{1}{2}$ft (60–75cm) tall Sensation Mixed, with flowers which keep open all through the day. The same applies to the 1ft (30cm) tall Nicki Mixed, an F_1 strain with an excellent colour range. The fragrance of the Nicki mixture is especially strong, this coming out fully, as with the tobacco plants generally, in the evening.

The range of marigolds, or *Tagetes*, is very wide, both in the African and the French types—the first including plants with heights of 1ft to 3ft (30–90cm), the second 6–10 inches (15–24cm). Good varieties of French marigolds include the 9 inch (22cm) tall 'Honeycomb' with golden-yellow and brown, double, crested flowers and the superb 'Queen Sophia' of similar height, which has fully double red blooms prettily margined with golden-yellow. The double-flowered Boy O' Boy mixture, height 6in (15cm), provides a mixture of colours, mahogany-red, golden-yellow, bright yellow and orange. If large blooms are to your liking then these you get in African marigolds like the Climax mixture, 3ft (90cm) tall, and the somewhat shorter 'Doubloon'. Gay Ladies mixture is but $1\frac{1}{2}$ft (45cm) tall and provides excellent blooms of orange, golden-yellow and yellow colouring. Of the Afro-French hybrids an outstanding F_1 hybrid is 'Nell Gwynn', with large mahogany-red centred golden-yellow flowers borne on 1ft (30cm) stems.

I remember how impressed I was when I first saw the compact-growing strain of *Tagetes signata pumila* named Starfire a few years ago. I am still impressed, for these 10 inch (24cm) tall plants provide a carpet of mahogany-red, golden yellow and lemon yellow with their tight-packed, small flowers. It is ideal for edging.

The perennial *Salvia farinacea* has a first-class variety named 'Victoria' which is grown to great effect as a half-hardy annual, and has been since its introduction in the late 1970s. It won a Floroselect bronze medal in that organisation's all-Europe trials in 1978. With its good foliage and bold spikes of violet-blue flowers borne on 2ft (60cm) stems, it is immensely alluring and is a plant for which many uses can be found in the garden.

The hardy biennials are a select little band which, for those who are prepared to take the trouble, have a great deal to offer. Sowing

Excelsior hybrids, a robust strain of the common foxglove *Digitalis purpurea* (see p. 60)

is done in a seed bed outdoors or in a cold frame during early summer to provide plants for transferring to a reserve bed and then moving to their flowering positions in autumn. One of the most useful and decorative of the biennials is undoubtedly *Cheiranthus allionii*, the Siberian wallflower, which produces its orange blooms on 1¼ft (37cm) stems from March until May and often until late June or early July. It has an excellent bright golden-yellow variety named 'Golden Bedder'. The *Cheiranthus cheiri* (wallflower) varieties come in heights from 6 inches to 1½ft (15–45cm) and in colours which embrace cream, yellows, many shades of pink, red and purple. These are fragrant, which the Siberian kind are not. One of the most effective of the taller kinds of wallflowers is 'Fire King', a bright scarlet, and another is 'Cloth of Gold', while of the low-growers mention must be made of the Tom Thumb mixture, some 9 inches (23cm) tall.

Of the foxgloves (*Digitalis*) the Excelsior strain still reigns supreme, producing its lovely blooms in July and August on stems some 5ft (1.5m) high. It is the exquisite markings on the blooms, in their varied colours of cream, shades of pink and purple, which give them special appeal—and the blooms are, of course, borne all round the stems. There is also a lower-growing mixture named Foxy (some 3ft [90cm] tall) which can be raised as half-hardy annual by sowing the seeds under glass in early spring. All foxgloves love light shade.

In pansies, too, there is much to delight the gardener, from the Roggli Giant mixture, 6 to 8 inches (15–20cm) tall, to the Clear Crystals mixture and the Majestic Giants. In sweet williams my choice would be the dwarf Indian Carpet strain with its excellent colour range and height of about 6 to 9 inches (15–22cm). This needs full sun to give of its best.

The hollyhock, *Althaea rosea*, is, of course, a perennial but it is best treated as a biennial, and that notable strain, Summer Carnival, 5 to 6ft (1.5–1.8m) tall, can even be grown as a half-hardy annual to flower in the first year. This strain has double flowers of good quality in colours from red and pink to yellow and white. Also widely available from seed houses is the admirable Chater's Double Mixed strain, with a good colour range and a height similar to the last.

Vegetables growing in a raised bed

Vegetables and fruit

What is surprising about vegetable growing is how much can be achieved in a small area. Cheap food is a receding memory, and on that score there is plenty of incentive to grow at least a little of one's food requirements. But the real pleasure for any gardener comes from growing and then enjoying at the table the best that the seedsman has to offer. The main problem is likely to be an aesthetic one. However well it is kept, a vegetable plot can detract from the overall effect of a garden, bearing in mind that it needs to be sited in an open position to give the good light which the majority of vegetables demand. On the other hand, it is often quite easy to provide a low screen which effectively overcomes the problem, either a fence on which permanent climbing plants can be grown, or, if a summer screen is quite sufficient, perhaps a row of french beans separating that part of the garden from the rest, Sweet peas or trained apples and pears can be used in the same way. The fact that quite of lot of vegetables can be successfully mixed with flowers should not be overlooked either. Vegetables can also look attractive grown in a raised bed.

Many herbs can be grown in containers, from mint (which needs restraining in any case), parsley and thyme to chives, which are always useful to have to hand.

It is most gardeners' ambition to have at least a few apples in the garden and possibly a few pears as well. If space is very tight then even dwarf bushes may be considered to take up too much room. So it comes down to trained specimens and of these the simple single-stem cordon is probably a better choice than the espalier form of training. Single-stem cordon apples and pears can be planted $2\frac{1}{2}$ to 3ft (75–90cm) apart in the row; trained on wires to form a screen between the vegetable plot and the rest of the garden they serve a very useful dual purpose. Apples need a good well-drained soil, not too heavy nor too light. Pears need rather warmer conditions to crop well and are not happy on heavier soils; they are more susceptible than apples, too, to frost damage at the flowering stage.

You must take note of the pollination requirements of whatever varieties you decide you would like to grow. Most apples are partially self-fertile, but for first-rate cropping there must be other compatible varieties nearby and flowering at the same time to effect cross pollination. On varieties, too, it is always a good idea to get local advice on which do well in your district.

If you have a south-facing wall with a clear space of 15ft (4.6m) or rather more, then consider growing espalier-trained pears —always allowing you have not earmarked this for one of the shrubs suggested earlier! For a north-facing wall, then it could be either a Morello cherry or a 'Victoria' plum; both are self-fertile.

If necessary, you can resort to growing most of the bush and cane fruits in containers, provided these are of large enough size; but clearly it is better to grow them in the open ground if this is possible. I would certainly try to find room for a couple of black currants—perhaps the mid-season variety 'Ben Lomond', heavy cropping and rather late flowering, which is helpful where frosts are concerned, or the later 'Baldwin'. Then there is the recently introduced 'Jet', a late-ripening variety which flowers late, with the advantage of missing the frosts—an excellent introduction from the East Malling Research Station. These are shallow-rooting and need a soil which will not dry out unduly while still being well-drained. Red currants, if you have room for them, can be planted at 5ft (1.5m) apart and I would suggest either 'Laxton's No. 1' or 'Red Lake', with the Dutch-raised variety 'Jonkheer van Tets' a strong contender for space with the first-mentioned, for these two are early cropping, with 'Red Lake' following on. Again, with space in mind, it is possible to grow red and white currants ('White Versailles' is the most freely available variety) as single or triple cordons. All do well in sunshine or light shade, but avoid sites open to cold winds.

If you can provide good soil (light soils are just not suitable) then the gooseberry to go for is 'Leveller', a yellow-fruited variety which you can use for both dessert and culinary purposes. More accommodating but susceptible to mildew is 'Whinham's Industry', another dual-purpose variety. 'Careless', the much-grown culinary variety, needs a good soil like 'Leveller' when it will crop splendidly, but it does make a large bush. Plant bushes 6ft (1.8m) apart each way.

Try and find space for at least a row of raspberries, the most rewarding soft fruit in my opinion. These do well in sunshine or light shade, given a moist, well-drained soil. Two varieties deserve special mention: the early 'Glen Clova' and 'Delight', which is a mid-season variety. Both are excellent croppers. However, 'Glen Clova' is susceptible to virus infection and for this reason should not be planted near other varieties. Then there is 'Zeva', a variety which can start to bear fruit in mid-August but which is mainly an autumn-fruiting variety, from September onwards. The plants should be set 1½ft (45cm) apart in the row.

Virtually everybody is interested in strawberries—at the con-suming end in particular! They are a good crop for small gardens

'Red Lake', a mid-season red currant with good flavour, is a heavy cropper

in any case, but especially so in view of their suitability for growing in containers of various kinds (which must, of course, be deep and wide enough to hold enough good compost to meet their needs). I'm thinking especially of the barrel method of growing which can be such an attractive feature on a patio or paved sitting-out area. There are also proprietary tiered polypropylene pots in which strawberries can be grown on a patio. An early-cropping variety to consider growing is 'Pantagruella', and 'Cambridge Vigour' is a second-early variety with good flavour. Of the perpetual-fruiting (or remontant) varieties which continue fruiting into October, 'Gento' is to be recommended for flavour. Planted in a plot, set the plants 1½ft (45cm) apart in rows 2½ft (75cm) apart. They need good soil, good drainage, and access to plenty of sunshine.

A water feature

A considerable contribution can be made to the garden by a water feature. The chances are that you will decide to have a glass fibre or plastic pool or one made from heavy-duty pool liner (synthetic rubber or PVC) rather than a concrete version. Concrete pools are excellent if correctly constructed, but if not are likely to be a worry with leaks after spells of very severe weather, when cracking can result. If you plump for the easier option there are some fairly obvious pitfalls to avoid. With a rigid glass fibre pool it is essential to make sure that the support it gets from the surrounding ground is even all round, for a full pool can be extremely heavy and stresses and strains of this kind on the structure must be avoided. The chief danger with pool liners is that a sharp stone might be left in the base which, when the pool is filled with water, will tear the material when the weight presses down. That kind of situation can be avoided by bedding the liner onto a layer of sand or by placing underneath it a layer of plastic sheeting. (For detailed advice see *Water Gardens* in this series.)

A mistake to avoid—as in garden-making generally—is over-planting, which can be disastrous with aquatics, both visually and culturally. Particularly does this apply to water lilies (nymphaeas). Make sure that you leave your chosen varieties with ample room to develop, and that you choose varieties suitable for the depth of water that you can provide. Two of my favourites are 'Rose Arey' and 'James Brydon', for which you need about a foot (30cm) of water, while the sulphur yellow *Nymphaea pygmaea* 'Helvola' is a lovely miniature variety for a mere 6 inches (15cm) of water.

For shallow water of about 2 to 3 inches (5–8cm) I would especially recommend the lovely 1½ft (45cm) tall *Iris laevigata* 'Variegata' which has cream-variegated leaves and blue flowers in June and July. There is also the reedmace, *Typha minima*, which makes clumps of grass-like foliage and bears brown flower heads in early summer. You can also grow the pretty bulrush *Scirpus tabernaemontani zebrina*, in water up to 6 inches (15cm) deep. This is often known as the zebra rush from the white and green banding of the stems, which rise to a height of 3ft (90cm).

You will also need to introduce to the pool oxygenating plants like the water violet, *Hottonia palustris*, to keep the water clear.